Dream Big Live Large

Tap into God's Abundant Favor
And
Supernatural Increase

Dr. Kathleen Abate

authorHOUSE®

AuthorHouse™
1663 Liberty Drive
Bloomington, IN 47403
www.authorhouse.com
Phone: 1 (800) 839-8640

Published by AuthorHouse 11/09/2018

ISBN: 978-1-5462-4397-7 (sc)
ISBN: 978-1-5462-4396-0 (e)

Print information available on the last page.

Any people depicted in stock imagery provided by Getty Images are models, and such images are being used for illustrative purposes only. Certain stock imagery © Getty Images.

This book is printed on acid-free paper.

PROFESSIONAL ENDORSEMENTS

In Dr. Abate's newest book, "Dream BIG, Live LARGE", you sincerely sense her genuine desire, passion and gifting for every person to experience God's Highest and Best!

She lays a great foundation both balanced and biblical, and a step-by-step process to enter into God's divine abundance and overflow!

Dr. Kathleen writes Practical, yet Revelational. She is personally transparent about her own journey yet shares how she's been powerfully transformed! Her book allows anyone anywhere to begin the amazing adventure of entering and experiencing the Favor of God!

I encourage YOU, the reader, to slowly take in and enjoy page by page, chapter by chapter, the wisdom that will help to develop you into one who "Dreams Big and Live's Large".

Pastor Dominic Russo, Senior Pastor
Oakland Christian Church
www.oaklandchurch.me

My husband Dominic and I have been honored to be Dr. Kathleen's Pastors. There's not a kinder heart and a more generous person, but what has blessed Pastor and I even more is Kathleen's hunger and passion to pursue God with all her heart and to gain the wisdom that comes from sitting at His feet!

We have witnessed a new strength, healing and wholeness that now excites us yet further as she shares the truths that have transformed her life!

My friend, it's not by chance this book has come into your hands. My prayer for you is that you would GROW as did our Lord Grew!

"And Jesus grew in WISDOM and stature, and in FAVOR WITH GOD AND MAN" (Luke 2:52 NIV)

Pastor Amira Russo, Senior Pastor
Oakland Church
www.oaklandchurch.me

DEDICATION

First and foremost, this book is dedicated to my Lord and Savior, Jesus Christ.

The one who saved my life more times than I can even remember in every possible way that a person can be saved: physically, emotionally and spiritually.

The one who healed me inside and out when I wasn't even aware I needed it.

The one who brought me from the back to the front and from the dark into His glorious, saving light.

The one who never left my side no matter what I did or how far I strayed from Him, even when I knew I was backsliding.

The one who transformed my heart and renewed my mind.

The one who suffered unimaginably, died a criminal's death, was buried, and then resurrected... for me and for every single human being all the way through history, up until now and into the future.

The one and only true living God, Jesus Christ, who inspired this book and supplied me with the ideas and passion for it.

This book is testimony to my belief in the gospel of Jesus Christ, of which I am not ashamed to speak of or witness about to the world in a form that will forever exist beyond my own lifespan.

Secondly, this book is dedicated to the two most precious gifts given to me by God, Steven Anthony and AnnMarie Kathleen. They are not only my children, they are my heart. I am honored to have been chosen by God to be their mother. It is both a privilege and a blessing that far exceeds explanation.

My children are living, breathing miracles. Before they were even born, an ultrasound revealed an abnormality in Steven's brain and one also in AnnMarie's left kidney.

Doctors said Steven would most likely be born mentally retarded and suggested that he be aborted. But through fervent prayer and strong faith, Steven's brain showed absolutely no signs of any existence of abnormality after birth. All glory and praise be to God Almighty.

Steven and AnnMarie were born 2 months premature, spending the entire 1st month of their lives in Neonatal Intensive Care with tubes and IV's sustaining them. AnnMarie underwent major surgery at 3 months old for the removal of 1/3 of her left kidney, and Steven underwent corrective bilateral hernia surgery at 6 months old. Both surgeries were a complete success, and neither one exhibited any signs of abnormality resultant from the premature birth. Glory to God

At the tender age of 3, Steven and AnnMarie experienced the fragmentation of their family, the difficulties of divorce and the challenges of having to grow up much faster than children should have to.

Yet, through it all, they persevered, adapted, and grew into the two most amazing human beings I know. They are strong and resilient beyond what they even realize, and they are destined for true greatness.

Steven and AnnMarie's lives parallel perfectly with the theme of this book as a message to each and every one of us: with determination, faith, persistence and adaptation to circumstances beyond our control, we can all exceed any expectation that this world would want to place on us.

Thirdly, I dedicate this book to Pastors Dominic and Amira Russo, the two Senior Pastors at Oakland Church in Rochester, Michigan. These two amazing individuals have taught me by example what it means to be the hands and feet of Jesus Christ. They are completely sold out to Jesus, and their lives personify this.

Their faith is unlike anything I had ever witnessed before. It never fails, never falters, never wavers. They do not judge anyone – ever. Bringing the lost to Jesus Christ is their life mission. They are anointed, appointed and chosen.

Oakland Church is Holy Spirit filled. The presence of God is palpable there not only during worship, but all the time. I believe this is because of the calling on the Russo's lives and what they have contributed in spirit and heart to the Lord, as well as, to the flock they sheppard. It is a true blessing to be a part of this incredible church.

Pastors Dominic and Amira Russo have taught me that God never gives up on us. They've demonstrated a passion for Jesus that I had never seen before. They've prayed for me, covered me and lifted me up to the Lord. They have helped to bring me to Him and to understand His deep love for me.

Now I want to do the same thing for each one of you reading this book. Know that Jesus loves you beyond what you could ever imagine. Know that He will meet you right where you are. He will stand by you as you learn and fall and get back up again. He will never leave you or forsake you.

He died for YOU. Even if you were the only person on earth, He still would've died just for you, and only you! That's how deeply He loves you! You matter to Him. His love for you is immeasurable.

You are His heart.

So, I dedicate this book to you, the reader, as well. I speak life into your divine health and prosperity. I pray you will apply the biblical principles laid out in this book to your own life. If you do, they will elevate your life to levels you've never imagined. God bless you on the journey to your God-ordained destiny!

TABLE OF CONTENTS

INTRODUCTION

Is the bible really written by men who heard from
God Himself or is it just stories and thoughts that
men wrote from their own hearts and minds?

This is a question that many people all throughout time have argued and debated. It may be the most controversial and longest-running debate in existence.

Some people believe that it is 100% authentic and real. They believe God Himself spoke to the author of each book who has written His words down at His direction. They believe God chose each author and guided what they wrote through visions, dreams and their own experiences.

"All scripture is God-breathed." 2 Timothy 3:16

Others believe that the bible is simply composed of stories or legend carried down through multiple generations by different men, and then written down.

These two beliefs are about as different as they can get. Those on both sides of the debate are quite convinced of their own stance. They passionately disagree with one another.

What everyone on both sides of this debate does agree on, however, is the fact that the answer to the question of whether or not the bible is 100% real is either yes or no.

One must believe that the entire bible is authentic or that the entire bible is not. It doesn't stand to reason that one or more of the stories in it would be true while the others would not. There is no gray area with something like this. It's either 100% real or it isn't.

If we believe that the bible is real and authentic, that it is in fact the Word of God, then we must believe EVERYTHING it says.

We cannot pick and choose the parts of it that we want to believe. We cannot pick and choose the parts of it that align with how we want to live our lives. We must believe it in it's entirety if we sincerely believe it's from God because God wouldn't write a partial truth. God IS truth.

> **"Jesus saith unto him, I am the way, the truth and the life: no man cometh unto the Father, but by me." John 14:6**

My personal truth is that as I progressed through my own journey with Jesus Christ, I finally took the time every day to read the bible and witness it's transformation in my own life, I learned that God is very precise, organizational, exact and intentional.

Every word in the bible is written deliberately and with divine purpose. Every sentence is there with a particular message of what God wants and needs us to know.

Everything in the bible, the Word of God, comes directly from God Himself.

> **"In the beginning was the Word, and the Word was with God, and the Word was God." John 1:1**

This means that every time we read our bibles, the Word, we're not just reading ABOUT God; we're actually spending time WITH Him!

Realizing this was life-changing. I finally understood that the bible is an actual living Word. What was said to the men and women during biblical times applies to each one of us today. Miracles that were performed during biblical times can be and are still performed today. Blessings of healings, peace, harmony and prosperity that were given to the men and women of biblical times are for each of us as well.

This is why our dreams must be BIGGER. We must not limit ourselves to what the world tells us we can do or have or about who we are. We are destined through Christ to live LARGE so that others can see the glory of God through us and want to be part of His church.

We must also be empowered to bless others and advance the Kingdom's agenda on earth. Building schools and churches, traveling to other nations to witness about the gospel of Jesus Christ or being able to sow seeds into ministries so they can grow and glorify God are some of the things God wants to empower us to do.

But if we're struggling or if we're broken emotionally and spiritually, how can we dream big and live large?

We equip ourselves with the strategies and authority given to each one of us in the Word of God. Everything we need is all there. After studying the Word of God for 1 ½ years, I experienced transformations in my heart and my mind that can only come from God.

It was undeniably life-altering for me. I can't even describe it in words. It was so beautifully and divinely orchestrated by God that I want to share it with you.

Everything I've written in this book is validated by quoted scripture from the Word of God, so you'll know that what I've written is coming from Him, not me. This book is not a "how to heal brokenness and rise up" book based on worldly ideas or human abilities. This book is a "matter of proven fact" book based on divine promises that come directly from the mouth of God.

Reading this book and adhering to the biblical principles quoted in it will elevate you to all that God has designed you to be. So you can have everything that He has for you which is so much more than you could ever imagine for yourself.

> **"Now unto Him that is able to do exceedingly abundantly above all that we ask or think, according to the power that worketh in us." Ephesians 3:20**

I wrote this book for YOU in hopes that you will elevate into your God-ordained destiny-level blessings. May the living God bless you in an unexpected way as you read it and absorb its powerful messages.

Let's get started.....

CHAPTER ONE
"The Struggle is Real"

It's human nature to want to help each other right?

Most people who have lived through a life-changing struggle and have come out on top would want to share how they survived it, in hopes of making things easier for someone else. Misery doesn't always love company. Helping others is what "paying it forward" is all about. This book is my opportunity to be obedient to God and to "pay it forward" to everyone who is struggling with something in their life that they want to overcome.

Struggles in this world are very real and very common. No one is immune to them. Everyone will struggle with something at some time in their lives. God even warns us of this.

> **"Here on earth you will have many trials and sorrows.**
> **But take heart, because I have overcome the world."**
> **John 16:33**

Maybe you've lived through the pain of personal betrayal, or

You've been through an acrimonious divorce involving a custody battle over your own children that restructured your entire life, or

An unexpected accident rendered you temporarily or permanently disabled so you went from the ease and abundance of wealth to the daily struggle of not knowing how you'd pay your bills, or

You've been emotionally and physically abused, maybe even having your life threatened, or

Maybe you've lived through ALL of these kinds of struggles, and you're searching for ways to rebuild your life and get it back on track. You need to know how to navigate your path, strengthen your heart, discern your environment and regain your peace.

These are all of the reasons why I've written this book. I have lived through every one of these struggles in my lifetime, and never expected any of them to happen to me. All I could do was hope that I'd find an inner strength to get through them.

> **"We can rejoice too, when we run into problems and trials, for we know that they help us develop endurance." Romans 5:3**

To be molded and transformed into whom God created us to be by the trials and struggles of life is God's divine plan for each one of us.

If you've gone through any of the trials I've mentioned or even something similar, then this book is definitely for you. It's for everyone who needs to know that there is a way up and out, and that way is Jesus Christ.

Going through life's struggles can make us feel beaten down by life and cause us to lose our direction or focus.

Maybe you've never been married, but you want to be. Loneliness may have taken a toll on you. You're tired of having all of life's responsibilities fall on your shoulders. As you look around and see how happy everyone else is, paired up and always together, you can't help but feel like something's missing in your life. Seeing older couples holding hands warms your heart but saddens you at the same time because you wonder if you'll ever have that, and if you're going to grow old all by yourself.

Maybe you are married, but you know that a divorce is eminent. You're living more like roommates than husband and wife. You no longer feel connected to one another. There is a distance present that has built an impenetrable wall between the two of you. Laughter and fun is a thing of the past, and you fear that one day soon you'll hear the words you never ever want to hear: "I want a divorce", or maybe you'll be the one saying it.

Maybe you've having to learn how to navigate your life with bills that you used to be able to pay easily, but now it's an impossibility. You're legally obligated to pay loans and a mortgage or rent based on an income that used to be your norm, but now everything has changed because you can't work like you used to. Your physical health is drastically different than what it used to be. Banks and loan institutions have no sympathy for your unfortunate circumstances. They require payment on your financial obligations or they will take back what you don't own. You're entire life could change. You could lose your home or be kicked out of your apartment or no longer have any means of transportation.

Maybe you've never been wealthy, but you were raised in poverty and just don't know how to get out of that cycle. You look to the world for the answer, knowing that your current circumstances will never get you out of the financial hole you're in. You have no idea how you will survive. You have little to no food in your refrigerator, and your diet has become nothing more than inexpensive, fast food because that's all you can afford.

Maybe you've thought of living in a domestic violence shelter after being abused because you're so scared for your life you don't want to remain living where you do. You don't know what it's like to feel safe anymore, and you don't know how you'll make it on your own. You're completely broken, damaged and bruised from the inside out. You can't wrap your mind around how you allowed someone to do this to you. You doubt your own sense of judgment and fortitude. You feel misunderstood and confused. You're so lost that you don't even know where to start or how to put your life back together, knowing you're so far away from where you thought you'd be.

I understand these situations, and I know how it feels to be broken, lost, scared and desperate.

After living through struggles that altered the path of my life, it didn't matter what I did or how much I tried to do things on my own, nothing worked. It was like an invisible wall had been put up between me and the success I once had.

If you have or are currently experiencing this, you know exactly what I'm talking about.

As I continued on this path, I questioned everything. How could the very same tactics that I had used to build so much success in the past not work at all for me now? It didn't make any sense to me until I realized that Jesus was teaching me some things and strengthening me for a bigger and better future. There were things that He needed me to learn in order to prepare me for His promotion and advancement.

God will never upgrade you to something you're not prepared to handle. He will always put you in a position for success, and never ever for failure.

Realizing this, I made the decision to submit to Him and to His process.

It wasn't until I made the decision to develop a deeply submitted, personal relationship with Jesus Christ that I began to see His divine favor in my life.

Developing that relationship takes time. It's a process involving a lot of change and discipline. A complete transformation of your mind and your heart must take place, but the process works if you allow it to and are patient and diligent enough to go through it.

Where I am today is a testimony to this process initiated and driven by the power, love and provision of Jesus Christ.

We're going to unfold this process one step at a time. But before we begin this success journey together, you have to first understand and wrap your head around the unstoppable potential you have through Christ Jesus.

CHAPTER TWO
"Understanding Your Potential"

Did you know that as a believer in Jesus Christ, you were created to live by means exponentially above what you could ever imagine?

You're supposed to be living so well that others look to you as a resource or inspiration to get to where you already are. In other words, you're supposed to stand out.

God created you to stand out. He created you to be different.

> **"And the Lord hath avouched thee this day to be His peculiar people, as He hath promised thee, and that thou shouldest keep all His commandments." Deuteronomy 26:18.**

To be "peculiar" is to be strange, unusual, unfamiliar and atypical. God declares that His people (believers) are unlike the masses. They are seen as being set apart because they do not live the way most people do.

The choices and decisions they make, they way they carry themselves and the way they speak differs greatly from those of the world (unbelievers).

Believers don't do things the way the rest of the world does. They do things that the world does not consider fun like going to church in the middle the week, studying the bible or going to church gatherings instead of going out dancing and drinking at the club. They don't use curse words, and they don't like gossip. These things are boring or too "goody goody" to the world, but they are fulfilling and important to the believer.

Believers also have an unexplainable peace within them. They remain calm in stressful situations. They don't generally flare up and yell or disrespect others when they are in a situation beyond their control. They are patient, kind, empathetic and subdued.

These qualities are deemed as weaknesses by the world when, in reality, they are born from strength and self-control. This self-control isn't totally foolproof, however, because we are all human after all. So no one, not even believers, can uphold these characteristics all the time without fail.

> **"For everyone has sinned; we all fall short of God's glorious standard." Romans 3:23**

The difference is that, believers will repent to Jesus and apologize quickly. They easily forgive others wrongdoings against them and speak blessings over those who betray them. Their first reaction to bad news or illness is to pray, not to fear. They have a calmness about them that appears to be unnatural to the world. These are some of the reasons why they are considered "peculiar" and set apart from unbelievers.

God places these "peculiar" characteristics within believers as an example of how He wants everyone to react and behave. He wants the world to see the "peculiar" nature of His children to spark an interest in others to want to become like that. He wants the world to see how much happier they could be if they took on the characteristics of the believer.

> **"Give me happiness, O Lord, for I give myself to you." Psalms 86:4**

God wants you to lead others to Him by example. You do this by excellent living grounded in integrity, honesty and high-standard ethics with the unshakeable peace and solid financial security that could only come from Him.

Making the right decision in those moments when only you and God will know what you've done is integrity.

Have you ever seen a pair of sunglasses or a wallet left behind in a public restroom and you were the only person in there? Keeping the sunglasses because you liked them or taking money out of the wallet and keeping it would not demonstrate integrity. But turning those items in to a Lost and Found untouched is integrity.

Even though no one would know what you've done, you've still done the right and honorable thing in the eyes of the Lord who will be pleased in you for doing so.

> **"The Lord detests people with crooked hearts, but He delights in those with integrity." Proverbs 11:20**

Even though no one but God would know about you doing the right thing, telling others the story of what you found and how you handled it is a great way to lead by example.

When it comes to honesty, being honest in business transactions is just as important as not lying to those you love. For example, if you're at the cash register in a store and you hand the cashier a $10 bill to pay for a $5 item, you'd expect to be handed $5 in change. But if you're given $15 back because the cashier thought you presented a $20 bill, honesty would cause you to assure the cashier that you shouldn't be receiving that much money back.

Even though the cashier thought you deserved the $15 in change, you know the truth and should be honest about it. Being dishonest would put extra money in your pocket, but it may cost the cashier his/her job when the drawer is reconciled at the end of the shift. It would appear to her superiors that she stole money because her drawer count would be short.

Although purposely short-changing someone might not be something you'd ever do, there are other more subtle ways that we can get caught up in dishonesty. Lying to those we are in personal relationships with is one of these ways. In fact, we can actually fall into it much easier than you might think. You don't have to lie about something significant for it to be considered a lie.

You could do something as simple as tell your friend that you prefer her new haircut when secretly you liked it better before. Obviously you don't want to hurt your friend's feelings, however you don't want to lie either because that's not righteous.

So how do you avoid lying to your friend but not hurting her feelings at the same time? Maybe you could just say that its "different" rather than actually saying you like it better than before. This would not be a lie. However, telling her that you love her new haircut when you actually don't would be a lie. It would also be fake. No one wants a fake friend, and God hates all lies, even the one's society considers "little white lies".

> **"Don't scheme against each other. Stop your love of telling lies that you swear are the truth. I hate all these things, says the Lord." Zechariah 8:17**

In actuality, there is no such thing as a "little white lie". Believing that "little white lies" are ok is a lie from the enemy who tricks us into being unrighteous. He will suggest to us that telling a lie for the purpose of trying to avoid hurting someone's feelings is kind and good. He will also propose that telling lies to avoid someone from getting upset is ok. But it's not ok because a lie is a lie no matter what. When you lie, you are bowing to the enemy, and he knows it.

> **"For you are the children of your father the devil, and you love to do the evil things he does.... He has always hated the truth because there is no truth in him. When he lies, it is consistent with his character; for he is a liar and the father of lies." John 8:44**

We obviously don't want to bow to satan. We want to bow to God in the way we live. So aside from having integrity and being honest, we need to live by a high-standard of ethics. This means that our behavior should positively affect those around us with respect, kindness and justice.

It means being faithful, kind and fair not only to those you're in a personal relationship with, but also to those with whom you conduct business. Everyone you interact with needs to know that you mean what you say and say what you mean without hidden agendas that benefit yourself over them.

So if you are selling a car, for instance, and you don't disclose specific information about its true condition, that would not be ethical. For example, you know that the car you're selling is going to need a new alternator but you also know that no one would really know that based on how the car is running. So you decide NOT to tell the buyer.

Trying to get more money off of a product you're selling by not disclosing its faults is wrong and unfair to the buyer who ends up paying more than the product is actually worth. Think about how you'd feel it you were the buyer.

The general rule of thumb needs to be, 'Treat others the way you'd want to be treated'. In fact, this is biblical.

> **"Do to others as you would have them do to you."**
> **Luke 6:31**

These biblical standards are something we must all aspire to live by daily. If everyone did this, imagine the kind of world we'd live in. People would actually want to reach out and help each other because they'd know that they would be treated the same way in return. This would be something that we would all make a conscious decision to do.

But what about the unshakeable peace that God wants us to demonstrate to others? This is not something that we do for ourselves, but rather something that God actually places inside of us when we sincerely seek Him.

Seeking Him means that you look to Him first whenever you're in a difficult situation. Pray to Him first; don't worry. Ask Him for guidance first; don't try to figure it out on your own. Lean on Him first; don't look to other people for worldly advice or assistance to help you, and thank Him in advance for what you need. Then, He will undoubtedly respond by placing within you a supernatural peace regarding your problem because He loves you and recognizes when His child truly reveres Him and is in need.

> **"Don't worry about anything; instead pray about everything. Tell God what you need, and thank Him for all He has done. Then you will experience God's peace, which exceeds anything we can understand. His peace will guard your hearts and minds as you live in Christ Jesus." Philippians 4:6-7**

There is no one and nothing on this earth that can solve any problem you have better than Jesus Christ. He created everything in existence and as such, He literally controls everything. He also knows things we don't know, and He sees the future. So He can solve things in ways that we can't even begin to imagine.

> This is why God said, **"For just as the heavens are higher than the earth, so my ways are higher than your ways and my thoughts are higher than your thoughts." Isaiah 55:9**

If God's solutions were things that we could come up with on our own, He wouldn't be God. Not only does He work on a supernatural level that our human minds could never fully comprehend, but He is extraordinarily clever and brilliant beyond our most intelligent thoughts.

He created everything in existence from the gigantic and limitless solar system consisting of complex orbital patterns of planets, moons, asteroids, comets and meteoroids down to the most miniscule microscopic electron particles of the atom which is the smallest unit into which all matter can be divided.

He did all of this, and everything in between, in just 6 days!

> **"God created everything through Him, and nothing
> was created except through Him." John 1:3**

Every living organism was designed and created by God to be dependent on another for survival. It's a genius system of checks and balances. God is a true genius.

These organisms comprise communities of balance wherein they sustain life and function to other communities of organisms. These are ecosystems such as forests, grasslands, deserts, tundra, freshwater and marine.

The various ecosystems work together to sustain human existence as well as animal food chains. Each living thing exchanges food and nutrients among others, passing energy from creature to creature.

Among all of the species created, (plants, insects, animals with spines (vertebrates), animals without spines (invertebrates), reptiles, amphibians, fish and birds, there are a total projected 50 million different kinds of species in existence today.

Each creature is comprised of microscopic cells made up DNA, deoxyribonucleic acid. DNA is a microscopic set of instructions that determines the exact specific look and characteristics of every creature. These instructions dictate eye color and shape, hair color, skin texture, the presence of scales, feathers, or fur, bone structure, the shape and size of bodies, the details of a face and every single characteristic that every single creature has.

So these instructions are ingenious genetic blueprints. These highly complex, yet microscopic, blueprints are designed to be like 2 rungs of a ladder made up of two smaller chains of molecules that actually click together and connect the two strands on a level so miniscule that it is unable to be seen with the naked eye. Every living creature has a genetic blueprint.

Are you beginning to see how astronomically complex and intricate all of this is and how unimaginably brilliant God must be to have created all of this?

"We can't even imagine the greatness of His power."
Job 37:5

If His brilliance to create everything in the universe is so incredible, then His power to do other things must also be much greater than we can ever explain.

God works on a divine, supernatural level. He supernaturally transfers His peace inside of us when we are troubled.

"And now, may God who gives us His peace, be with
you all. Amen." Romans 15:33

This peace is a gift from God that serves to direct us to the right path and remain strong in the right frame of mind as we are dealing with the difficulties of this world.

The enemy creates chaos and stress in our lives. Chaos and stress block the mind from being able to focus, and they cause confusion, or "brain fog". That's why you can't think straight when you're extremely stressed out, or in distress. You generally can't sleep well either.

Eating food is also affected. You either can't eat at all because you're nauseated or you eat way too much because you're trying to numb the stress and make yourself feel better. On top of all that, you're so fearful of the consequences of whatever your situation is that you're on emotional overload.

It's debilitating to say the least.

On the other hand, God keeps us focused on Him to allow us to receive His strategies, ideas and courage in order to get through the most difficult of circumstances. He clears our mind and calms us. He offers us something the world cannot – His healing peace.

> **"I am leaving you with a gift – peace of mind and heart. And the peace I give is a gift the world cannot give. So don't be troubled or afraid." John 14:27**

God wants us to be able to navigate through our lives easily. He also wants to eliminate the fear and uncertainty that is directly attached to financial instability.

After all, how can you feel joy and want to praise Him when you're consumed with worry?

If you're afraid of being kicked out of your home or apartment because you don't have the money to pay your mortgage or rent, it's difficult to relax and enjoy life. In fact, it would be difficult to do anything other than think about the fact that you can't make the payment. You'd be trying to figure out where you're going to go and what you're going to do.

So poverty and financial instability is not the way God would have you live. He desires for ALL of your needs to be met.

> **"And this same God who takes care of me will supply all your needs from His glorious riches, which have been given to us through Christ Jesus." Philippians 4:19**

This includes your financial needs as well. Because if you don't have money to live, how does that glorify Him?

Food, shelter and clothing (bare necessities) cost money. So because we live in a world that uses money for the exchange of goods, we need money in order to navigate in this world.

In addition to being able to support ourselves, if we don't have money to bless others and help others in need, that doesn't glorify God either.

Building homeless shelters, centers for kids and churches costs money. So in order to bless others with the things and places that are necessary for their well-being or will nurture their spiritual growth, we need money, as well.

The more you bless others, the more you will receive from God. The basic principle of divine exchange is that when you give, you receive.

God will reward you with a spiritual blessing or a financial one when you are generous with what you have because what you have is what He has given to you. It's His, not yours.

He expects you to give to others and not to keep it all for yourself. When you give money to bless others, the more you give away, the more God will give back to you.

> **"Give freely and become more wealthy; be stingy and lose everything." Proverbs 11:24**

Many people believe that God doesn't reward His children with money because money is evil. But this belief is not biblical. According to God's word, it isn't money that's evil; it's the LOVE of it that is. Money in the hands of the righteous becomes a blessing to others. But money in the hands of the unrighteous becomes an idol and ends up being more loved and endeared than God.

> **"Dear children, keep away from anything that might take God's place in your hearts." 1 John 5:21**

> **"It is better to be godly and have little than to be evil and rich." Psalms 37:16**

Understand that God will give and He will take away when and how He decides to. He pays careful attention to how His children handle what He's given to them. This includes money.

Make no mistake about it, money is provided to us by our Abba Daddy. It is not provided to us by our jobs. Our jobs may be the medium through which God gets money to us, but it is God who is the actual Provider. This is so important to grasp.

God gives us everything we have that is good, including money.

> **"God gives wisdom, knowledge, and joy to those who please Him. But if a sinner becomes wealthy, God takes the wealth away and gives it to those who please Him." Ecclesiastes 2:26**

God is Jehovah Jireh. The Hebrew meaning of this is 'the Lord will provide'. This is why even though you may not have earned a promotion or a raise, you still got one. Or why a fellow worker might receive favoritism from the boss and it seems unfair.

You see, God can cause your boss to promote you or demote you. He can cause you to get a raise or a bonus. He can cause you to get fired. God can cause your business to boom at an unnatural rate. He can send you new customers if He desires to; or He can block new customers from your business if He desires to redirect your focus. He has a plan for your life and He will do whatever He deems as necessary in order to move you, guide you and direct you towards His plan.

> **"You can make many plans, but the Lord's purpose will prevail." Proverbs 19:21**

In reality, your job is merely the platform upon which you are supposed to build and strengthen your "real" job which is your calling, or purpose, through Christ Jesus.

> **"I cry out to God Most High, to God who will fulfill His purpose for me." Psalms 57:2**

As long as you are honoring Jesus Christ in your everyday life and decisions and putting Him first, it doesn't matter what your job is. God will provide all of your needs. Whether you're a janitor, a waitress, a doctor, a lawyer or a painter, God will supply you with riches when you demonstrate that you love Him with all your heart and put Him first place in your life.

"Those who love me will inherit wealth. I will fill their treasuries." Proverbs 8:21

But He isn't a genie in a bottle passing out money to those who wish for it. He is your God who sees your heart and knows when you sincerely love Him, and when you have good intentions to use money to bless others.

You can't fake it. He knows the condition of your heart. If you seek Him in greed, you will not be blessed with financial overflow.

"Seek the Kingdom of God above all else, and live righteously, and He will give you everything you need." Matthew 6:33

A great example of righteous seeking of the Lord was King Solomon. He loved and honored the Lord with all his heart and sought Him first for counsel above anything or anyone else. He asked to be given great wisdom, so he could carry out his role as King in the most honorable and fair way to those he ruled.

So God distinguished him. God gave Solomon great wisdom and great wealth too. He became the most wise and wealthiest man in history. It was well known by everyone who knew him that his financial well-being had been blessed directly by God. There wasn't another man who had the wealth Solomon had. He was admired. Others were awestruck by his tremendous wealth.

God desires to do the exact same thing with you, and He wants you to tell others that He is the reason for it all. He wants everyone to know that there's no way you could've ever achieved what you have at the level which you have, unless it was Almighty God who blessed you.

"Now unto Him that is able to do exceedingly abundantly above all that we may ask or think, according to the power that worketh in us." Ephesians 3:20

But in order to receive such a blessing you must have your heart and mind aligned with Jesus Christ.

CHAPTER THREE
"Aligning Yourself with God"

*How can we be sure that God will bless us the same
way He blessed Solomon?*

God is no respecter of persons. What He did for Solomon, He will do for you. All you have to do is align your heart and mind with Jesus, live righteously and make blessing others a priority. What He does for one righteous believer, He will do for every righteous believer.

It doesn't matter if you live in Italy, Africa, Japan, Honduras, Australia or the United States. It also doesn't matter if you're a man, a woman or a child; nor, does it matter what color skin, hair or eyes you have.

> Peter said, **"I see very clearly that God shows no favoritism. In every nation, He accepts those who fear Him and do what is right." Acts 10:34**

What matters is that you acknowledge Him as your Lord by surrendering yourself to Him completely and choose to live righteously. The question is: how do you surrender yourself to God? The answer is: you must get yourself out of your own way.

What does this mean? How can you get yourself out of your own way when you live with yourself and with your own thoughts and feelings? Our thoughts and feelings are what makes us who we are. They define our actions. They also define how we react to others and how others see us.

If our thoughts, feelings, actions and reactions are defined by worldly standards or expectations, then we are allowing ourselves to be defined by the world, and not by God. The world becomes the standard against which we measure ourselves rather than God.

The key to getting ourselves out of our own way is for God to become our standard instead of the world, so our actions and reactions are aligned with His.

For example, the world says that a man who cries is weak. In response to this, some parents teach their young boys to be strong, to be tough and not to cry when they're upset, in order to teach them how to suppress "weak" emotions.

These parents look to the world for validation rather than God. They don't want their son to be judged by the world. Society's opinion of their son ranks higher than letting their child express himself freely and naturally. It's a "suck it up, buttercup" cold-hearted attitude designed to create a strong man in they eyes of the world.

When this is what's taught to a young boy, it could very likely have a detrimental effect on him. He could grow up to be insensitive and incapable of empathizing with others when he sees them cry. This is because he's been conditioned by the standards of this world to view this as a weakness.

He may even secretly resent that he was never able to express sadness in a natural way. He may have even built up a resistance or suppressive mechanism to the emotions that would cause him to cry. This would inevitably change who he is in his own heart and mind, and he would probably begin to see others through "different eyes". He may view those who cry as weak and not strong because that's what he was taught.

So the way he views others and the way he views himself is skewed toward the expectations of the world rather than those of God. This is dangerous because the way we view things directly reflects the way we behave.

"Their minds are full of darkness; they wander far from the life God gives because they have closed their minds and hardened their hearts against Him." Ephesians 4:18

This same boy who grows up into a man and views others as weak may gain a false sense of superiority to others. He may become cold, arrogant and prideful. He may treat others with insensitivity and rather than reaching out to help those in need. His view may be that they should help themselves because their own weakness put them in the position they're in. If this is his view and it affects his behavior, then it means he is judging others.

He may not even be capable of recognizing that sometimes bad things happen to good people. Judging others isn't of God. It places false barriers and division between people. This is one of the devil's favorite tactics; pride and division.

The enemy doesn't want us to help one another, but rather to put ourselves first and to view ourselves as better and more important than others.

"So letting your sinful nature control your mind leads to death. But letting the Spirit control your mind leads to life and peace." Romans 8:6

So you see, in this case, a person who is taught to conform to the world's standards can end up unknowingly partnering up with the devil rather than with God.

When our thoughts do not align with God's thoughts, then our hearts don't either. And the things we do and choices we make come from the condition of our hearts and what's inside.

"And do not be conformed to this world; but be ye transformed by the renewing of your mind, that ye may prove what is that good and acceptable, and perfect, will of God." Romans 12:2

You may reside in this world, but when you are a child of the Most High God, you are not of it. You're just in it.

Getting yourself out of your own way means simply to conform to the perfect will of God in the things you think, say and do rather than thinking, saying and doing what you want to do or what makes you feel or look better to the world.

If a car cuts you off while driving and comes within inches of hitting your car, and then the driver puts his or her hand out of their window to give you profane gestures, you'd probably feel inclined to pull next to that driver and say something (yell something) or drive as close as you possibly could to their back bumper to make them upset because they've just upset you. 'Tit for tat', right?

That's a natural reaction to an unexpected and extremely upsetting event. But it's also a worldly reaction that gives a foothold to the enemy through anger.

> **"Human anger does not produce the righteousness God desires." James 1:20**

God's preference is for you to take the high road and just go about your business and forget about it, allowing that driver to keep moving and drive away. This may seem cowardly to some people, but it actually requires great discipline. It takes strong discipline to restrain yourself in a situation like this.

But the enemy is counting on you to be weak. He wants you to react without discipline because he knows that when you are weak, he gets strong. Your weakness allows sin to creep in and then the door is wide open for him to interfere with your life any way he wants to.

Some of the ways he enjoys interfering with your life is to block your financial income, cause strife in your marriage and other relationships, cause you to lose sleep and interject destructive or self-deprecating thoughts into your mind.

When you sin and open the door for the enemy to interfere in your life, it's like you've just invited him and his demon gang to come inside your home and join you for coffee, set up camp and move right in with you and your family.

Sinning is going against the perfect will of God. When this happens, it means that a spiritual law has been broken. This will, by the law of heaven, allow the enemy to accuse you in heaven's court before God Almighty.

The enemy is watching and waiting all the time for something to accuse you about. His agenda is to populate hell and he wants you there too.

> **"One day the members of the heavenly court came to present themselves before the Lord, and the accuser, satan, came with them. "Where have you come from?" the Lord asked satan. Satan answered the Lord, "I have been patrolling the earth, watching everything that's going on." Job 1:6-7**

So be careful not to give the enemy an open door into your life. You must make the conscious decision to be led by God and not this world. Get your emotions out of the equation. Align your thoughts, your words, your actions and your heart with the perfect will of God. This must be an intentional act on your part.

> **"Clothe yourselves with the presence of the Lord Jesus Christ. And don't let yourself think about ways to indulge your evil desires." Romans 13:14**

How do you know what the perfect will of God is? It's all in His Word. He has laid it all out for us so we know exactly what to do in every situation. If you read your bible but still don't know how to handle a particular situation, then ask God what to do in prayer. He will always meet you where you are and meet your needs when you seek him earnestly and with a pure heart.

> **"For everyone who asks receives. Everyone who seeks, finds. And to everyone who knocks, the door will be opened." Luke 11:10**

God will never leave a prayer unanswered. He is always listening to you, looking at the condition of your heart and waiting for you to align yourself with Him so He can take you higher.

However, before He takes you to new heights in your life, He must first prepare you to ensure your success on the mountain top. God will always raise you up for success because He loves you and wants you to flourish. He wants you to be triumphant.

Just know that God is not a genie in a bottle who grants our wishes without us having to do anything. There is a process to God's preparation of us for elevation and promotion which requires some hard work and patience on our part.

CHAPTER FOUR

"It's a Process"

*Isn't it true that anything truly worthwhile in
life takes both time and preparation in
order to receive it?*

Earning a doctorate degree requires several years of study. It takes a minimum of 8 years of training beyond high school and requires absorbing an exuberant amount of information. The title of doctor establishes someone as an expert in their particular field of study. A doctorate degree can be earned in Medicine, Psychology, Economics or in any field.

A doctor needs to know everything about their field of study. They must graduate with a specific GPA and pass a nationwide examination before the title can be bestowed to them. There is no way to circumvent this process. However, it's the process that is responsible for the transformation of a student into an established professional.

So the process absolutely works and is a good thing.

Other areas of life require preparation and time as well. Having a baby is another example. Babies aren't birthed after just a few weeks of fertilization. This new life requires several months in utero to develop and grow. During the first 3 weeks, cells join together to become an embryo with nerve cells. Then everything else forms, limbs, organs skin etc., until the fetus has fully developed and is ready and able to survive outside the womb. This process takes 9 months.

During these 9 months, the parents-to-be are also preparing for their new roles. They will be going from doing what they want whenever they want and having nothing tying them down to being 24 hour/7 days a week caregivers, protectors and nurturers of a helpless little human being who requires assistance to eat, burp, bathe, walk and to do everything. They will have to put the needs of the baby above and before their own.

This is a life-changing responsibility. The gestation period of the development of the baby becomes an adjustment period for the parents-to-be. After the birth, there are new demands on finances as well as new sleep schedules that replace the familiar ones. Day-to-day time tables must be restructured and reorganized too.

Preparatory periods, or processes, are an important part of any upgrade in life. They are carefully designed and structured in every area of life, so we can benefit from the time and training required to be able to properly handle what we're going to receive.

It's no different with the elevation or promotion of God. If you desire to walk in the favor of God with financial overflow, preparation for that is also necessary. Until you're a good steward of the money you already have, God will not release more to you. He will need you to be prepared to receive more so you handle it properly and spend it wisely when it's actually in your hands.

God will always set us up for success. He does this by introducing and releasing things to us in small steps, and ensuring that our emotional and spiritual maturity level is where it needs to be before releasing more to us.

He is our Abba Daddy. He wants the best for us. He's protective over us. So He won't allow us to do things we aren't prepared for.

We're the same way with our children.

Would you allow your 8 year old to drive your car? Or would you want your teenager to prepare your friend's taxes just because he's getting an A in accounting class? No. You'd want them to be ready to do those things and prepared and properly trained with the right mindset and skills to be victorious and successfully help others.

Preparation in the spiritual realm is unlike that of this world. In the world, most people need to have a degree or a particular skill set that has been taught and honed in order to be successful financially. But this is not the case with God.

With God, a cook and a doctor can have the exact same amount of money in the bank because titles mean absolutely nothing to Him. What matters to God is your heart and your obedience. If you're an obedient blood-washed, born-again child of God, sky is the limit for your finances because God will meet you right where you are and elevate you to wherever He wants to be.

He can cause your business to soar in the worst of economic conditions. He can cause the dealership to lease you a car with bad credit. He can inspire someone to gift you with money. He can download innovative strategies to you for your business and cause you to meet the right people to bless your ministry.

He can even supernaturally place money in to your bank account. This has actually happened to me. True story! My bank account jumped up thousands of dollars overnight. Only God's divine favor can do something as incredible as that. But in order for Him to do this, He must see that you are prepared to receive it, and that your faith is where it needs to be for you to believe it.

So, yes, there is preparation required to receive God's favor in financial overflow, but it's not the same kind of preparation that the world has conditioned us to expect. It's internal preparation, not external.

God's preparation starts with aligning yourself with His thoughts, actions and words and ends with the alignment of YOUR heart with HIS. This is what will put you in good standing with the Lord. Because when you're heart is in the right condition and you respect God enough to never want to displease Him, obedience will follow.

> **"I have hidden your word in my heart, that I may not
> sin against you." Psalms 119:11**

So loving God will keep us from sinning against Him and being disobedient. This act is so important that God has actually commanded it.

> **"Jesus replied, "'You must love the Lord your God with
> all your heart, all your soul, and all your mind.' This is
> the first and greatest commandment." Matthew 22:37**

Aligning yourself with God is a process. It's a process unlike any other, though. The process occurs supernaturally, and it is found in the Word. So you must familiarize yourself with it. Read it every single day without fail. Study it. Allow it to prepare you and do a work in you.

> **"If only you would prepare your heart and lift up your
> hands to Him in prayer." Job 11:13**

In doing this, you'll begin to feel a supernatural transformation taking place because nothing you do on behalf of God is ever wasted or without return. Reading His Word is spending time with Him. He blesses His faithful children who seek Him. When you put Him first, He will take care of you in ways you've never imagined.

> **"Seek the Kingdom above all else, and live righteously,
> and He will give you everything you need."
> Matthew 6:33**

Everything you need means EVERYTHING from job promotion, to marriage, to unexpected financial windfalls, and even little things like maybe getting a purse you've been wanting. God cares about every little thing you desire. He rejoices in making you happy.

Remember that He is parental with us, and rewards His children based on their actions and thoughts just like we do for our own children.

If your child takes special care to do his household chores, puts tremendous effort in his schoolwork and is polite and loving, aren't you more motivated to gift him with things that make him smile? Don't you sometimes want to get him a little something extra for his birthday as a reward?

Well that's exactly how our Abba Daddy is with us. He is parental. We are His kids and He absolutely adores us beyond what we could ever wrap our limited, finite human minds around. He will give us what we desire when we are obedient to Him, and His favor will prosper us.

> **"May He grant your heart's desires and make your plans succeed." Psalms 20:4**

When God begins to do things like this in your life, your love for Him will deepen because what you'll be seeing in your life will become very personal to you. He will become more real to you than He ever has been before. It's not that you'll love Him more because He's giving things to you with favor. It's that you can feel Him becoming personal with you, and His presence around you becomes palpable.

The length of time that this process takes is different for everyone. So be patient. Know that He loves you more than words can ever describe, and He wants you to prosper far above what you even imagine.

> **"And may you have the power to understand, as all God's people should, how wide, how long, how high, and how deep His love is. Ephesians 3:18**

As you go through the process and transformation of your mind and heart start happening, you'll find that although you are living in a physical world, you are operating in a spiritual one. You are making choices that please God, and you are receiving your validation from Him rather than from people. Loving Him and being obedient to Him will become your priority.

> **May you experience the love of Christ, though it is too great to understand fully. Then you will be made**

> **complete with all the fullness of life and power that comes from God. Ephesians 3:19**

As a result, you will see that raising you up to levels far exceeding anything this world can provide will become His priority because that's what's in His heart to do for you. You just have to do your part for Him to release it to you.

> **Now unto Him, who is able, through His mighty power at work within us, to accomplish infinitely more than we may ask or think." Ephesians 3:20**

When you make God your priority, He will make particular blessings and provisions for you His priority. The anointing flows through the presence of true faith, however. That's the key to actually receiving what He has for you to advance you to the next level of blessings.

CHAPTER FIVE
"Faith is a Currency"

If money is required to move goods in the physical world, what's required to move favor and blessings in the spiritual one?

Faith is the currency of God. Faith is defined as the complete trust or confidence in someone or something. Having faith in God means you know beyond any shadow of a doubt that you can count on God, and you believe with all your heart that He will move on your behalf even before you actually see it happen.

"Now faith is the substance of things hoped for, the evidence of things not seen." Hebrews 11:1

This is supernatural stuff, and that's why it's so powerful.

We're so conditioned by this world to only believe in what we can see, touch, taste, smell or feel. Our minds tell us that in order for something to be real, it must be able to be recognized by one or more of our five senses.

This is a lie straight from the pit of hell. It's one of the most popular tools used by the enemy to fool people into thinking that they can only believe in or count on the things that are palpable.

You can't see, touch, taste, smell or feel faith. It's not a visible or palpable thing. It's a spiritual currency that exists only in our hearts and minds when we know who we are in Christ, and we know exactly who He is. Realizing His supreme power, mighty authority and formidable significance is what will create faith in a believer. And faith is supernatural power that affects physical things.

> **"And Jesus said unto them, if ye have faith as a grain of mustard seed, ye shall say unto this mountain, remove hence to yonder place; and it shall remove; and nothing shall be impossible unto you." Matthew 17:20**

Right here, Jesus says that nothing will be impossible for those who have faith. This is exactly why the enemy tells us that everything invisible or impalpable isn't real. It's the most effective way for him to keep us from having faith and reaping its rewards. He knows the power that faith has in the spiritual and natural world. So if he can stop you from using faith, then he can stop you from receiving the promises and favor that God designated for you before you were even born.

> **"But without faith, it is impossible to please God; anyone who wants to come to Him must believe that God exists and that He rewards those who sincerely seek Him." Hebrews 11:16**

Faith moves God. That's what is meant by it being a currency in the spiritual world. It's a medium of exchange. Without it, you will not experience Him breathing on your life with the abundant favor that is only unlocked with faith. With it, you will experience things that are supernatural and miraculous.

> **"You can pray for anything, and if you have faith, you will receive it." Matthew 21:22**

> **"Then He touched their eyes and said, 'Because of your faith, it will happen.'" Matthew 9:29**

> **"Daughter, He said to her, "your faith has made you well. Go in peace." Luke 8:48**

"And Jesus said, 'Stand up and go. Your faith has healed you.'" Luke 17:19

"And Jesus said, 'All right, receive your sight. Your faith has healed you.'" Luke 18:42

Miracles are something most people want to believe in, but if we're being honest, they don't really believe in them unless they've actually received one or have actually "seen" one happen to someone else. This is because miracles can not be scientifically explained or proven, so they're difficult to believe in.

Even the most extraordinary things can be explained with some kind of scientific phenomenon. Like the way water can boil and freeze at the exact same time. This is a phenomenon because boiling water and freezing water exist at two completely different extreme temperatures.

So how can this be possible? It occurs when the temperature and pressure is just right for the three phases of a substance (gas, liquid and solid) to coexist in what's called a thermodynamic equilibrium. More specifically, it's termed the "triple point".

So this phenomenon can be explained in scientific terms, proven by experimentation in a laboratory and written about by scientists and as such, is easy to accept and believe.

What about the extraordinary phenomenon of supernatural healing?

A few years ago, there was a 9 year old girl from Texas that was miraculously healed of 2 life-long incurable diseases that several different doctors claimed would take her life at a young age.

She was diagnosed with Pseudo-Obstruction Motility Disorder and Antral Hypomotility Disorder which could be seen on radiographs and professionally diagnosed.

This little girl had suffered from excruciating pain, multiple hospital admissions and tubal feedings since she was only 5 years old. Her stomach was so severely distended (swollen) that she couldn't eat food because her intestines couldn't digest it. Although her condition was medically proven to be fatal, her father had faith in God's healing power and her mother never gave up on her.

She was constantly in and out of hospitals for tests and intravenous medication administration. Her childhood had been hijacked by the enemy for 4 years. The emotional strain and pain she experienced daily became so overwhelming that she even wanted to die. No matter what doctors tried to do to make her feel better, nothing worked.

Then one day, destiny knocked on her door, while she was home with her family. She went outside and decided to climb a tree and accidentally fell 30ft into the hollow center of that tree where she remained for 5 hours until she was finally rescued and air-lifted to the hospital. Her family prayed for her and believed that she was not dead. Neighbors came in droves to witness her rescue and pray along with her family.

A fall like that should've taken her life, but by the grace of God, she survived. When she regained consciousness, she said she had seen Jesus, and He told her she was healed. Suddenly all of her symptoms were gone. Doctors could no longer find any trace of either of these diseases on her radiographs when the evidence was clearly seen on them prior to the accident. It was like the diseases never even existed in her body.

Her healing couldn't be explained by any scientific means or tests. Her doctors couldn't explain what had happened.

Scientific evidence of the diseases existing on Xrays and Cat Scans, along with her swollen stomach, inability to keep food down and daily pain, proves that she had the diseases. But what about the scientific evidence showing how these 2 incurable diseases disappeared? There is none.

We know beyond any doubt that these 2 diseases were gone because they were no longer "seen" on radiographs or "felt" by her. They were incurable diseases, but if they would've somehow been cured by any treatment there would've been a dissipation or lessening of the radiographic signs or symptoms experienced by the little girl. But this wasn't the case at all. The diseases just suddenly and totally disappeared.

This was an invisible and impalpable miracle that cannot be explained by worldly terms. But we believe it happened because we can test and "see" that the diseases are gone.

This incredible miracle made national news and was written into a movie called "Miracles from Heaven", starring Jennifer Garner. It was released in 2016. This movie is a testament to how God's power is moved by faith.

Today, this little girl remains healthy and healed from both of the fatal diseases that robbed her of 4 years of her life. She is a living, breathing miracle.

Her destiny was that she was going to be healed, but God often works on multiple levels at the same time. His plan was to heal her while increasing the faith of everyone who would hear her story on a national level. Faith is the key that unlocks destined doors.

Just like He did when He saw the faith of everyone praying for this little girl, God steps in when He sees our faith. When God steps in, He shows out in a big way. There is nothing questionable about His miracles or His power. He could've healed her anytime during any one of her hospital stays or while she was put on new medications or treatments. But He chose to do it following a fall that would've killed anyone.

He wanted everyone to know beyond any doubt that He not only miraculously saved her life from the fall, but also miraculously cured her of 2 incurable diseases. He showed Himself in a mighty way to her family so they could believe in His miracle and strengthen their faith, along with everybody else's, by telling the world about it.

Faith in the supernatural healing power of Jesus and other miracles is unexplainable, but also very real.

Believe in the promises on your life and the desires in your heart and you'll receive them. Faith moves God. He created you. He can do anything He wants. He can heal. He can cause opportunities to appear to you. He can increase your finances. He can bring you your Boaz or Ruth. He can change people's minds. He can cause second chances to come back around again. He can give you favor in the courtroom. He can save your marriage. He can cure your addiction. He is God Almighty.

When you have faith and believe in the unseen, God will cause you to see your miracle, favor or blessing in the natural. He works in the supernatural to affect the natural.

> **"By faith we understand that the entire universe was formed at God's command, that what we now see did not come from anything that can be seen."**
> **Hebrews 11:3**

The entire universe being formed at God's command literally means that God spoke the universe in to existence. Isn't that remarkable? So speech has divine, supernatural power. Let's talk about this....

CHAPTER SIX
"The Power of Speech"

*Did you know that the very same power in the words
God used to speak the world into existence is in your
words too?*

The spoken word is superior to anything written or silently read. It has within it the power to create, to bless, to curse, to break demonic bondages and to deliver people from demonic attacks of all kinds. It has authority over the entire atmosphere and everything that exists within it, physical and spiritual. The spoken word is what God used to create the world and every single thing, living and nonliving, that exists in it.

> **And God SAID, let there be light; and there was light."
> Genesis 1:3**

> **"And God CALLED the light day, and the darkness He CALLED night. And the evening and the first morning were the first day. And God SAID, let there be a firmament in the midst of the waters, and let it divide the waters from the waters." Genesis 1:5-6**

> **"And God CALLED the firmament Heaven. And the evening and the morning were the second day. and God SAID, let the waters under the heaven be gathered together unto one place, and let the dry land appear; and it was so. And God CALLED the dry land earth;**

and the gathering together of the waters CALLED He Seas: and God saw that it was good. And God SAID let the earth bring forth grass, the herb yielding seed, and the fruit tree yielding fruit after its kind, whose seed is in itself, upon the earth: and it was so." Genesis 1:8-11

"And God SAID, let there be lights in the firmament of the heaven to divide the day from the night; and let them be for signs, and for seasons, and for days, and years." Genesis 1:14

"Then God SAID, "Let lights appear in the sky to separate the day from the night. Let them be signs to mark the seasons, days and years. Let these lights in the sky shine down on the earth. And that's what happened." Genesis 1:14-15

"Then God SAID, 'Let the waters swarm with fish and other life. Let the skies be filled with birds of every kind." Genesis 1:20

"Then God blessed them, SAYING, 'Be fruitful and multiply. Let the fish fill the seas, and let the birds multiply the earth." Genesis 1:22

"Then God SAID, 'Let the earth produce every sort of animal, each producing offspring of the same kind- livestock, small animals that scurry along the ground, and wild animals. And this is what happened." Genesis 1:24

"Then God SAID, 'Let us make human beings in our image to be like us..." Genesis 1:25

"Then God blessed them and SAID, 'Be fruitful and multiply. Fill the earth and govern it. Reign over the

fish in the sea, the birds in the sky, and all the animals that scurry along the ground." Genesis 1:28

"Then God SAID, 'Look! I have given you every seed-bearing plant throughout the earth and all the fruit trees for your food....and this is what happened." Genesis 1:29-30

God could've created the world any way He chose to. He could've looked at things to create them if He wanted to. But He chose to SPEAK everything into creation. And He chose to make sure we knew the power of that by putting it in His Word.

What does this mean for each and every one of us? It means that this is a power that we need to tap into if we want to tap into the divine destiny, the mind-blowing favor, the pre-planned promises and the extraordinary blessings that God has for each one of us.

Understand that our words carry in them the very power of God because the air in our lungs is from God. His breath becomes our life. Our breath is God's power.

"Then the Lord God formed the man from the dust of the ground. He breathed the breath of life into the man's nostrils, and the man became a living person." Genesis 2:7

God wants us to be certain to carefully craft our words. Our words can unleash legacy-sized blessings or block them. Our words can send demons packing or invite them to come live with us. Our words can claim victory or succumb us to defeat. Our words can restore brokenness or hinder healing. Our words can bring us life or cause death.

"Death and life are in the power of the tongue: and they that love it shall eat the fruit thereof." Proverbs 18:21

What kind of death and life is being referenced here? ... every kind. Spiritual death and life, physical death and life, the death and life of a business, financial stability and influx, a marriage, a family bond, an idea, a strategy, a dream, a promise and a destiny are all being referenced in this very telling scripture.

This scripture must be well understood in order for our BIG dreams to manifest into the LARGE life that God has planned for us. So we are going to break it down and carefully discuss all of the different kinds of death and life that we can experience as a direct result of our speech. Not knowing what this scripture really means is often times the ruination of divine progression and growth.

> **"My people are destroyed for lack of knowledge: because thou hast rejected knowledge, I will also reject thee." Hosea 4:6**

Some people elevate to the levels God has for them, while others get stuck in a bad rut for the rest of their lives. That's not going to be you.

CHAPTER SEVEN
"Spiritual Death and Life"

*Is it possible to be a slave to sin and to be
saved at the same time?*

Yes, it is possible. It's also very common. Many believers all over the world read their bible and pray every day. But they don't live by what they know to be truth, according to the Word. So they're partnering with the enemy rather than God. They're captive to sin without even realizing it.

By definition, a slave is a person who is the legal property of another. If you've given the enemy a foothold in your life or opened the door for him to enter your life by sinning, then you have become a slave to sin.

**"Jesus replied, 'I tell you the truth, everyone who sins
is a slave of sin." John 8:34**

You have inadvertently given the enemy the legal right to attack you. There is no gray area when it comes to who you bow to. You can't bow to Jesus and to the enemy at the same time. When you sin, you are bowing to the enemy, even though you may believe in your heart that you only bow to Jesus Christ.

You see, whether you realize you're sinning or not, doesn't negate the fact that you've done it. The enemy will accuse you in the heavenly court of what you've done, and if he can prove that accusation to be true, he will be given access to you as a result.

41

> **"And I heard a loud voice saying in heaven, 'Now is come salvation, and strength, and the kingdom of God, and the power of His Christ: for the accuser of our brethren is cast down, which accused them before our God day and night.'" Revelation 12:10**

The good news is that if you are a blood-washed born again believer, you have the authority through Jesus Christ to rebuke the enemy, repent and break the bondage in Jesus' name.

The key is recognizing the traps the enemy puts in front of you, and understanding that knowing the Word isn't enough to protect you against his attacks.

Maybe you read your bible every day and you can even recite some versus. Maybe you give to the poor and volunteer your time to help those in need. Maybe you're a good, kind person who tries to do right by others. Maybe you love the Lord and pray a lot and go to church on Sundays.

These are all good qualities and acts, however, if you do all of these things but you don't allow the Word of God to seep deep down into your soul, submit to it whole-heartedly and obey everything it tells you to, then you may unknowingly allow the enemy to steal your favor.

God's favor is not free. This may seem unfair, but it's not.

Favor is given to those who earnestly seek after the Lord, and to those who make a conscious effort to put Him first all the time, while consistently obeying His commands. It's given to those who have an unshakeable confidence that certain blessings will be released to them as a result of their unstoppable pursuit of Jesus, in the way that they live their lives.

The Word of God is "seed" in our lives that we must cultivate, fertilize and water with obedience and submission to Jesus. Then the good "fruit" (abundant favor of God) will be brought about from that seed.

When seeds are planted in the ground, if they're planted in good soil, then the seeds are able to take deep root, thrive and grow into what they were created to become. They will produce something much larger than the original small seed from which they came. They might grow into a 100 ft tree or a beautiful blooming flower with multiple flowers or a large leafy plant with clusters of grapes.

In other words, if we allow the Word of God to transform us in our hearts and minds, then a destiny much BIGGER than we could've ever imagined for ourselves will become our reality.

But if these same seeds are planted in soil that is nutrient deficient, then they will not become what they were meant to become. They may be smaller than they were supposed to be or they may die.

Our dreams die and never become our reality when we do not conform ourselves to the Word of God. Even the enemy knows the Word. He can quote scripture just like many believers can. So it's living the Word of God that will make a difference in your life, not just knowing what it says.

The spiritual seeds we sow can either multiply our blessings or block them. They can give us eternal life with Jesus or destine our souls to hell.

Jesus explained it beautifully in a parable to His disciples. We need to let what He said sink in and apply it to our lives.

"The farmer plants seed by taking God's Word to others. The seed that fell on the footpath represents those who hear the message, only to have satan come at once and take it away.

The seed on the rocky soil represents those who hear the message and immediately receive it with joy. But since they don't have deep roots, they don't last long. They fall away as soon as they have problems or are persecuted for believing God's Word.

The seed that fell among the thorns represents others who hear God's Word, but all too quickly the message is crowded out by the worries of this life, the lure of wealth, and the desire for other things, so no fruit is produced.

And the seed that fell on good soil represents those who hear and accept God's Word and produce a harvest of thirty, sixty, or even a hundred times as much as had been planted!" Mark 4:14-20

So the key to the growth and full potential of the seeds is dependent upon the soil in which it is planted.

The exact same thing is true in our lives. If we don't "plant" (adhere to) the Word of God with all of His commandments and spiritual laws deeply into "good soil" (a fully submitted flesh willing to obey God), then those seeds will not produce the favor of God in our lives that God had available to us before we were even born.

The enemy doesn't want you to access the abundant favor of God because he knows that when you receive that favor, you will become unhindered. You will be a true threat to his kingdom. He doesn't want you to become a warrior for Jesus Christ and bring others to salvation. His goal is to populate hell with as many people as he can. The favor of God is what will empower you to fund the Kingdom of God, strengthen the Kingdom of God and to populate it.

Populating the Kingdom of God is your main objective while you're here on earth. It's the great commission. The enemy works overtime to keep you from that commission by stressing you out, blocking your finances, causing strife in your relationships, keeping you distracted from God's ideas and hindering your destiny.

The enemy doesn't really care how many times you go to church or how much you volunteer to help others or even if you read your bible. He cares about whether or not you actually do what it says and fully submit your flesh to its laws and commands.

The enemy will work through weak and wounded people to try to cause you to fall into sin. Even if the sin is very minor in your eyes, he can get a foothold into your life. Sin, no matter what kind it is, no matter how serious or frivolous it may seem to be, will open the pathway to the enemy's taunting and keep you from what God has for you, So do not fall prey to it. You must discern the enemy's tricks and traps.

He can be very cunning. It takes the discernment of the Holy Spirit to recognize the tricks of the enemy. Jesus warned us to be wise.

> **"Behold, I send you forth as sheep in the midst of wolves; be ye therefore wise as serpents, and harmless as doves." Matthew 10:16**

Why did Jesus reference us to sheep and the enemy and his minion, fallen-angel workers as wolves? Wolves eat sheep. They hunt them. They search for them with determination, pursue them, and then they kill them. Wolves are predators and sheep are their prey.

This is exactly what the enemy does to us, isn't it? His objective is to not only kill our chance for being with Jesus for eternity but also to kill our joy, love, happiness, dreams and destiny while we're still here on earth. He actually has a three part agenda that never changes.

> **"The thief's purpose is to steal, kill and destroy." John 10:10**

It's important to understand that spiritual death and life isn't limited to the final destination of our soul after we have died. Certainly, in that regard, if you have spiritual life after death, then you will not die and you will live with Jesus for eternity.

Likewise, the death of your spirit would mean that you would not enter heaven, but rather burn in the firey lake of hell for eternity with the enemy.

But spiritual death and life also refers to our spiritual condition and how that can affect what we see happening in our natural lives. When the Holy Spirit puts a "super" on our "natural", then the physical world in which we live can be affected in a very positive way.

CHAPTER EIGHT
"Physical Death and Life"

*How does the spiritual world collide with
the physical world to produce miracles
that can be seen with the natural eye?*

God created every physical and spiritual thing in existence. Your body is merely a temporary physical housing for your inner spirit. You are in all actuality, a spiritual being made in the image of God.

> **"So God created human beings in His own image. In the image of God He created them: male and female, He created them." Genesis 1:27**

So when you are born again, you enter a process of internal overhaul wherein you are redeemed, renewed and transformed by the Holy Spirit on the inside to take on the characteristics of Jesus Christ. In actuality, you are a spirit temporarily residing within a human body assigned to you by God. This body you reside in while here on earth is a temple of God. It belongs to God, not to you.

> **"Don't you realize that your body is the temple of the Holy Spirit, who lives in you and was given to you by God? You do not belong to yourself" 1 Corinthians 6:19**

Through faith, God's supernatural power can heal any physical ailment of your body. God made you. He made all of your internal organs, your arms and legs, your head and brain etc. He created and designed you Himself. So if your kidney fails, He can give you a new one. If you lose an arm in an accident, He can grow you a new one. He can restore your damaged eyesight, your hearing and your speech. He can do it all and more because He is Jehovah Rapha. In Hebrew, this means, the God who heals.

> **"And He said, 'if you will listen carefully to the voice of the Lord your God and do what is right in His sight, obeying His commands and keeping all his decrees, then I will not make you suffer any diseases I send on the Egyptians; for I am the Lord who heals you."**
> **Exodus 15:26**

This divine power of healing requires your faith to operate in the physical world. You must "speak life" over your healing and release your faith into the atmosphere in your own words because words have creative power through Christ.

You "speaking life" over your body for healing, gives the angels around you the opportunity to do their job. They're waiting on you to initiate the healing in confident faith with your words, and when you do this, healing will happen. It's supernatural. God puts His superior (super) power and authority over the physical (natural) imperfections and diseases of the world when you operate in faith.

On the other hand, if you "speak death" over your healing, then you will not be healed. "Speaking death over yourself is something that can happen without you even realizing that you've just cursed yourself. The power of your own words is that fateful.

Here's an example: if a doctor has just told you that you've been diagnosed with cancer and you have 3 months to live, you can't repeat that diagnosis, saying, "I have cancer and I have 3 months to live." Releasing that into the atmosphere is a curse against yourself. It's not biblical truth. So if you declare the lie over yourself, then that's what will be. Speaking a lie over yourself will block divine healing power from reaching you. You must speak biblical truth over yourself always.

Even though the doctor said those words to you, they are a lie from the pit of hell. God does not lie.

> **"God is not a man, so He does not lie. He is not human, so He does not change His mind." Numbers 23:19**

He has not put anything in the bible that is not true or only partially true. So if the Word says you are healed and whole, then you are healed and whole. Your belief in that is critical.

> **"When Jesus saw her, He called her to Him and said unto her, 'Woman, thou art loosed from thine infirmity." Luke 13:12**

Jesus' words to this woman are for each of us. He is no respecter of persons. If she was healed, so are we. That is truth.

Not only is it important for us to understand that we are all healed because Jesus said it, but we also need to pay very close attention to exactly what He said to her. He said that she was loosed from her infirmity. That means that she had been delivered from the disease. So disease comes from demons.

Disease, or infirmity, is not of God nor is it from Him. He does not inflict disease upon us. He made us in His own image. God is not weakened, unsound or unwell, and neither are we.

> **"So God created human beings in His own image. In the image of God he created them; male and female He created them." Genesis 1:27**

Disease is evil. It is not biblical truth. As such it can be rebuked and removed from you as long as you do not accept the disease with your words and make it your reality or your own personal truth.

Always speak truth over yourself and not the lies of this world. The enemy is very cunning in the ways he often gets us to curse ourselves unbeknownst to us.

You must verbally declare with your own words that you are healed and whole and that nothing the enemy throws your way will harm you. In order for your words to have healing power, you must be born again, living righteously and obeying the Lord.

Whenever you are under attack, say this scripture out loud with confident faith in your heart:

> **"No weapon formed against thee shall proper; and every tongue that shall rise against thee in judgment thou shalt condemn. This is the heritage of the servants of the Lord, and their righteousness is of me, saith the Lord." Isaiah 54:17**

Be mindful not to speak other lies that are so commonly thread into our everyday speech that affect the quality of your life. Growing old does not mean that you take pills, ache all over and can't do anything. Those are all lies from the devil.

How many of us have relatives that go downhill health wise as they age? They talk about the doctor's appointments they have, the procedures they're having done and the medicine they take. They accept the conditions that they've been diagnosed with by naming and claiming them without realizing that's what they're actually doing. In fact, this becomes the focus of many of their conversations. They unknowingly curse themselves over and over again. As a result, their physical conditions not only remain, but also get worse over time. This is not at all what God intended.

Growing old is a gift and a privilege. Not everyone experiences it. You were not meant to spend the latter years of your life in agony. You are made in the image of God. Growing old in the eyes of God means gaining wisdom and joy, not senility and misery.

Do not believe the lies this world tells you about aging, and do not speak them over yourself or they will become your reality.

Lastly, it's important to break any word curses said by others against you as well. This includes word curses that you may not even know about. Others may not understand spiritual law and healing according to God's word and truth. They may speak word curses over your healing without even meaning to. Maybe they even talk about the disease you've been diagnosed with amongst other people, speaking life into it.

You have the authority through Christ to break word curses off of you. Do it daily, knowing that Christ lives in you, and so does His power.

> **"...And this is the secret: Christ lives in you. This gives you assurance of sharing His glory." Colossians 1:27**

Christ living in you means that His power resides there too. With His power, you can speak life into anything that the bible promises you.

God promises for you to be healthy, and He also promises for you to be wealthy. All you need to know is how to tap into it.

CHAPTER NINE

"Death and Life of Business or Finances"

*Would you agree that money problems
are directly linked to anxiety and depression?*

Dealing with money problems is a very serious matter. For some people, it causes sleep depravity, irritability and such a high level of stress that it's hard for them to even get out of bed.

It can become physically and mentally debilitating. Body aches, self-deprecation and depression are commonly associated with serious financial struggle. These conditions can actually become so significant that they can end up requiring professional attention.

You see, it's not simply the lack of having enough money to buy the niceties, it's worrying about the electricity being shut off or having to take cold showers because the gas company turned off the shutoff valve outside the house.

It's dreading the never-ending phone calls from collection companies wanting money you may not have to pay bills that are seriously delinquent.

It's having a scarce pantry of food and an empty refrigerator, and desperately craving to eat things you can't afford to buy.

It's hoping the gas in your car will get you all the way to work without turning off in the middle of the intersection because you know the tank is almost empty, but you don't have the money to put more gas in it.

It's the fear of not being able to send your kids to college or being kicked out of your home for not paying the taxes.

These kinds of money problems are beyond stressful, and that's just the way the enemy wants it. He wants you completely overwhelmed and under an extraordinary amount of pressure. He wants the stress to steal your joy.

He wants you focused on your problems, your deficits and your fears. He wants you to be so low in the ground emotionally that you start believing the lies he begins telling you about how worthless you are and how humiliated you should be. He wants you to be so depressed that you can't praise God. When this happens, he has succeeded in getting you right where he wants you: breaking spiritual laws.

Fear, worry and self-pity are ungodly. These emotions are spiritually debilitating. They block your favor. They are offensive to Jesus who died for you to be able to live in abundance and not to fear anything. Jesus said this:

> **"My purpose is to give them a rich and satisfying life."**
> **John 10:10**

He promises to give us everything we need. It is not God's intent for any of us to be in need of anything. Paul said to the Philippians:

> **"And this same God who takes care of me will supply all of your needs from His glorious riches, which have been given to us in Christ Jesus." Philippians 4:19**

God wants all of our needs to be met so we can go out to spread the gospel to others.

> **"And He saith unto them, 'Follow me, and I will make you fishers of men.'" Matthew 4:19**

This is our true purpose. We all have a different platform (job) from which to do this, but the common thread is to grow the church and advance the Kingdom of God in the battle of soul winning between Jesus and the enemy.

This is indeed a great commission. It requires provision. Finances are needed to travel to other countries and teach people who have never heard the name Jesus Christ who He is and what He's done for us. Money is required in order to build churches and schools. In order to be able to provide those in need with food and clothing, these things must first be bought.

Jesus intends for us to live well and to not have to think about how our needs will be met but instead, to focus on Him and obeying His commands, blessing and loving others.

> **"But don't be so concerned about perishable things like food. Spend your energy seeking the eternal life that the Son of Man can give you. For God the Father has given me the seal of His approval." John 6:27**

Since money problems are so distracting from our servanthood to God, it's often the most popular way the enemy keeps believers from the life they are meant to have. The truth is this:

> **"Now unto Him who is able to do exceedingly abundantly above all that we may ask or thing according to the power that worketh in us." Ephesians 3:20**

This means we are called to live above any way of life we can even imagine for ourselves. Exceedingly abundantly means tremendously plentiful. It means that all of your basic needs are met and then on top of that, you have extras that you don't need at all, but you get to enjoy them. This is your portion. This is your inheritance. It's right in the bible.

Why then do so many believers not have it?

It must be spoken out of your mouth as truth. It must be declared as something you expect as your inheritance as a child of the Most High God. Even when your bank account balance shows $0 and even when your business is running slow or in the negative, you must speak life into the situation.

If you're not speaking life into your situation, then you're speaking death into it. Complaining and stressing about financial strain does not cause God to move in your life because the power that is working in you is sin, not thankfulness.

The truth is that you're either speaking life or death over your situation. There is no gray area. You're speaking one way or the other depending on whether or not you believe in your heart that God's promises to you are actually yours.

If you speak exactly what you see in the natural, then you're cursing yourself and blocking your own inheritance. But if you speak what your truth is as it is stated in God's Word and promises, and you truly believe that God is a promise-keeper, then you will see a divine change and God will be begin to move on your behalf.

Remember that God is your Jehovah Jireh. Depend on Him only. Do not depend on your paycheck, your business or your job. When you depend on Him to pay your bills and eliminate your debt, He will. Jesus already paid all of your debt for you on the cross. He doesn't want to see you struggling to make loan payments to people or banks or lenders. You were not created to borrow. You were created to have such an over abundance that you will lend to others, not the other way around.

"The Lord will send rain at the proper time from His rich treasury in the heavens and will bless all the work you do. You will lend to many nations, but you will never need to borrow from them." Deuteronomy 28:12

So depend on Him to provide for you with confident faith, speak life into your wealth, and be sure to remain righteous and obedient to Him. These are the keys to unblocking financial strain.

If you do these things consistently and you have still not elevated, then one of two things is happening: it's not time for your elevation yet or there is a stronghold that must be delivered from you.

God is very precise, organized and structured. He will never set you up for failure. If you have more preparation to do, then He will not release your breakthrough until He knows you're ready to receive it. He has to know you are faithful and successful with little before He will give you more. This is His setup for success.

He wants to know that you will use your overflow and wealth to bless others and not spend it frivolously. He knows that if you are a good steward of what little you have, you will be a good steward of more.

> **"And if you are untrustworthy about worldly wealth, who will trust you with the riches of heaven?" Luke 16:11**

He wants to know that you want to elevate in order to honor the Kingdom because you love Him and not because you love money. You can't love God AND love money. You either love Him or you love money.

> **"No one can serve two masters. For you will hate one and love the other; you will be devoted to one and despise the other. You cannot serve God and be enslaved to money." Matthew 6:24**

To be enslaved by money means that you don't want to part with it. It means you're not generous with it. For some people, they feel it's hard to come by and they're not sure how long it'll take to get more. so they hold on to it, hoarding it. Others are just selfish with it and enjoy watching their bank account grow. And then there are the people who feel a sense of entitlement that it's theirs and they worked hard to earn it, so they aren't very excited about the idea of giving it to someone who may not have worked as hard or at all.

But what we all have to understand is that any money we have in our possession actually belongs to God, not us. God's financial blessings to us are weighed based upon the generosity we demonstrate with the money we already have. So if we are very generous with our tithe or donations to charitable organizations or ministries, then God is very generous with us when He gives us a financial blessing. Likewise, if we give a little, He gives us a little.

> **"Give, and you will receive. Your gift will return to you in full-pressed down, shaken together to make room for more, running over, and poured into your lap. The amount you give will determine the amount you get back." Luke 6:38**

Money is the currency on earth that is used for food, shelter, clothing and entertainment. But faith is God's currency. Money means absolutely nothing in the Kingdom of God. You can't take it with you when you die. It's temporal.

Everything money can buy is temporal. But eternal things like love, hope and faith can't be bought with money. These are the things that progress, transform, bless and elevate our walk with God.

> **"Three things will last forever – faith, hope and love – and the greatest of these is love." 1 Corinthians 13:13**

So timing is key with God. It is one of the most common reasons that some believers find themselves waiting for breakthrough long after they feel they should've already received it.

The other reason could be that there is a stronghold of poverty or financial strangling that has attached itself to you from an open door of generational sin passed down to you from generation to generation or from a door of sin you opened yourself.

The python demon is a snake that will strangle your finances and your business. It must be verbally rebuked in the name of Jesus. And then you must tell your mountain (the financial strain) about who your God is and take back its power.

God's power resides in you. Tap into it. Know that God's power inside of you is superior to the enemy and any demon in the world.

> **"And The Lord shall make thee the head, and not the tail; and thou shalt be above only, and thou shalt not be beneath" Deuteronomy 28:13**

God created the enemy and the demons that work for him. God will always reign over them. This means you will always reign over them too.

Learn this scripture and recite it often:

> **"..greater is He that is in you, than he that is in the world." John 4:4**

Today's culture has normalized some of the sin that is clearly laid out in the Word as sin. So you need to make sure you're following God's laws rather than man's laws when you're making decisions.

First of all, manipulation of any kind is witchcraft. Marrying someone that God did not send to be your spouse is not God's plan for you. Stepping outside of God's timing for your calling and trying to make things work on your own is not God's plan for you either. The world will tell you that you need to make things happen for yourself. That is a lie from the pit of hell. Don't buy into it.

Waiting on God's perfect timing will bless your endeavors. Being impatient will not. He sets the time for everything.

> **"For everything there is a season, a time for every activity under the sun.**
> **A time to be born and a time to die.**

A time to plant and a time to harvest.
A time to kill and a time to heal.
A time to tear down and a time to build up.
A time to cry and a time to laugh.
A time to grieve and a time to dance.
A time to scatter stones and time to gather stones.
A time to embrace and a time to turn away.
A time to search and a time to quit searching.
A time to keep and a time to throw away.
A time to tear and a time to mend.
A time to be quiet and a time to speak.
A time to love and a time to hate.
A time for war and a time for peace."
Ecclesiastes 3:1-8

All of these things bow to God's timing, so we must as well.

Second of all, disobedience of any kind is against God. Complaining, worrying, cursing, gossiping, unforgiveness, impatience and anger are all things we might fall prey to without realizing how rebellious they actually are.

This is so important. We need to examine each of these....

Complaining demonstrates unthankfulness for all that God has done for us. The Israelites were in awe of the supernatural parting of the Red Sea and so happy about being led towards the Promised Land, but then began complaining about how long it was taking to get there. That's unbelievable. How could they have witnessed such a magnificent phenomenon and then doubted God to finish what He started?

Complaining is self-centered. It shows God that we are not humbled by His great power and majesty. God is Omnipotent. He deserves our praise, not our attitude. Complaining angers Him.

"Soon the people began to complain about their hardship, and the Lord heard everything they said.

Then the Lord's anger blazed against them, and He set a fire to rage among them, and He destroyed some of the people in the outskirts of the camp." Numbers 11:1

Worrying about tomorrow dishonors God because, like complaining, it keeps us from thanking Him for all of the amazing blessings in our lives. It reveals doubt in our hearts about God's ability to help us. Worrying about the future is unappreciation for what God is doing for us in the present.

"So don't worry about tomorrow.." Matthew 6:34

Bask in the blessings of today because you can't see all that God is doing in the spiritual realm to align things up in your favor and get things ready for your imminent breakthrough.

Cursing others or using cursing language is disrespectful and dishonoring to the Father. There is power in our speech. God designed it this way. So to use that power in an evil way is like a slap in the face to God.

"You must not dishonor God or curse any of your rulers." Exodus 22:28

"And so blessing and cursing come pouring out of the same mouth. Surely, my brothers and sisters, this is not right." James 3:10

Gossiping may seem harmless, especially if the person being spoken about can't hear what is being said about them. But it's not harmless. It's unrighteous. Gossiping is a form of judgment against others whom God has created and designed Himself. If you criticize them, then you're criticizing God.

"Don't speak evil against each other, dear brothers and sisters. If you criticize and judge each other, then you are criticizing and judging God's law. But your job is to obey the law, not to judge whether it applies to you." James 4:11

Unforgiveness blocks our favor with God. It's like we are putting ourselves in a high-ranking seat of judgment against those who do us wrong, as if we rule over them. Forgiveness is not ours to withhold from others. It is something that God has actually commanded us to do. He will not tolerate us disobeying His laws.

> **"If you forgive those who sin against you, your heavenly Father will forgive you. But if you refuse to forgive others, your heavenly Father will not forgive your sins." Matthew 6:14-15**

Impatience demonstrates to God a lack of self-control to endure our circumstances. It's an act of subtle and indirect complaint. Without patience, we express a lack faith in God, and we can't build the stamina necessary for our breakthrough.

> **"Supplement your faith with a generous provision of moral excellence, and moral excellence with knowledge, and knowledge with self-control, and self-control with patient endurance, and patient endurance with godliness..." 2 Peter 2:5-6**

Anger is a very common sin. It's so easy to feel angry when others disrespect us or are inconsiderate toward us. In an age when selfishness is at an all time high, anger is close at hand. We have to learn how to repress it and not allow it to affect our thoughts, words or actions in order to do right by God.

> **"Human anger does not produce the righteousness God desires." James 1:20**

Selfishness is putting our own wants and desires for our lives above God's. For example, knowing that pre-marital sex is not biblical, but doing it any way just because you want to will put you out of alignment with God. Marriage was created by God as a sanctified union between a man and a woman. Anything else is not God's plan for your life.

> **"While the man slept, the Lord God took out one of the man's ribs and closed up the opening. Then the Lord God made a woman from the rib, and brought her to the man.**
>
> **This one is bone from my bone and flesh from my flesh. She will be called woman because she was taken from man.**
>
> **This explains why a man leaves his father and mother and is joined to his wife; and the two are united into one." Genesis 3:21-24**

If you put your children before God, your spouse before God, your money before God or anything before Him, you can be accused by the enemy in the heavenly court of worshiping an idol and being disobedient to God's command. This can basically invite the enemy into your bank account, your business or in any other area of your life.

> **"...if you love your son or daughter more than me, you are not worthy of being mine. If you refuse to take up your cross and follow me, you are not worthy of being mine. If you cling to your life, you will lose it; but if you give up your life for me, you will find it."**
> **Matthew 11:37-39**

God must be first place in your life before anyone or anything else. He deserves that honor. If you do this, He will reward you in all ways, including wealth.

> **"Seek the Kingdom above all else and live righteously, and He will give you everything you need."**
> **Matthew 6:33**

God's rewards are unlimited and all-inclusive. He can bless any part of your life with just one touch. Even relationships that seem to be hopeless and dead can be resurrected by our King Jesus.

"To all who mourn in Israel, He will give a crown of beauty for ashes, a joyous blessing instead of mourning, a festive praise instead of despair." Isaiah 61:3

CHAPTER TEN

"Death and Life of a Marriage or Family Bond"

Would you agree that family is the glue that holds everything in our lives together?

In a literal sense, family is the lineage from which we come. Our lineages have ancestral roots and places of origin. They define who you are in the natural.

Families often share specific characteristics, physical traits and similar interests. They help to carry us through the stresses of life. They give us strength, and they support us. Our families are a soft place for us to fall when things aren't going well.

The family structure was created by God to carry us through life and give us a natural, earthly example and understanding of the spiritual family of which we are a member of.

God is our Father. He is our Abba Daddy. When you are born again, you are adopted into the Kingdom of God as His child.

> **"... you received God's Spirit when He adopted you as His own children. Now, we call Him, 'Abba Father.'"**
> **Romans 8:15**

His dealings with us are parental in nature. He loves us and rewards us for making righteous decisions which sometimes are accompanied by personal sacrifice.

For example, if your friend betrayed you by going behind your back and dating your boyfriend, you'd naturally be upset with your friend and your boyfriend, wouldn't you? I mean, it'd be difficult to forgive them for something that was thought out and planned, especially when they knew it would be hurtful to you.

Maybe a part of you would even want to hurt them back. But instead you decide to forgive them both and then end your relationship with them. You pray for them to come to Jesus and carry on with your life without vengeance or anger in your heart.

This is personal sacrifice with a righteous reaction. This behavior will be rewarded by God.

> **"But even if you suffer for doing what is right, God will reward you for it." 1 Peter 4:13**

Likewise, if you do not react righteously in your circumstances, God will corner you to get you back on the correct path for your life just as a parent would because He loves you. It's His desire for you to be successful and happy.

> **"For the Lord disciplines those He loves, and He punishes each one He accepts as His child." Hebrews 12:6**

Jesus is our Intercessor to the Father. His Father, God, is also ours. So Jesus is our brother, our sibling. He is Lord, but also man – the Son of God. We, as sons and daughters of God are part of the royal family of God and King Jesus when we are born again. Together we make up the church.

> **"And we are members of His body." Ephesians 5:30**

Jesus is the head of the church, and we, as born again blood washed believers, make up the body of the church. This is our true family.

Our spiritual and earthly families give us a sense of belonging making us feel connected to something. Desiring to feel loved, needed and wanted is something that God has placed inside each of us. He wants us to feel obligated to loving and blessing others, whether they are part of our bloodline or not because we are all members of the same family. He commands us to love others as ourselves and to treat one another with sincere kindness and good intentions.

> **"This is my command: Love each other." John 15:17**

> **"Love each other with genuine affection, and take delight in honoring each other." Roman 12:10**

> **"A second is equally important, 'Love your neighbor as yourself." Matthew 22:39**

In fact, He even commands us to love our enemies, the ones who betray us, come against us and harm us.

> **"You have heard the law that says 'Love Your Neighbor' and hate your enemy. But I say, love your enemies! Pray for those who persecute you! In that way you will be acting as true children of your Father in heaven. For He gives His sunlight to both the evil and the good, and He sends rain on the just and the unjust alike. If you love only those who love you, what reward is there for that?" Matthew 5:43-46**

If we want to be forgiven by God for falling short of His righteousness, then we must forgive others.

> **"If you forgive those who sin against you, your heavenly Father will forgive you. But if you refuse to**

forgive others, your Father will not forgive your sins."
Matthew 6: 14-15

Unforgiveness builds walls between people and divides them from one another. It isolates them. God doesn't want us to be alone or isolated because there's power in numbers. The enemy understands this power, so he works tirelessly to isolate us from one another because it's much easier for him to attack us and play minds games with us when we're alone.

"A person standing alone can be attacked and defeated, but two can stand back-to-back and conquer. Three are even better, for a triple-braided cord is not easily broken." Ecclesiastes 4:12

One of the enemy's favorite strategies is to divide and conquer. It's very easy for him to do and it actually works the majority of the time. Its high success rate can be attributed to pride which he places in our minds and hearts. If we accept his "bait", then he wins the battle and fights relentlessly to keep it going.

When one person holds unforgiveness in their heart, and the other one is too prideful to apologize because they aren't the one in the wrong, division is born. Then all the enemy has to do is keep those emotions going strong in order to control the outcome. He will persistently remind each person of the hurt that occurred and the fact that it is undeserving to them. This is pride.

Pride is detested by the Lord because it separates us from Him. It selfishly pushes the Lord out of our hearts, creating within us a sense of entitlement which leaves absolutely no room for Him to work. So He will leave us to do as we will to do until we humble ourselves before Him.

"And when they cry out, God does not answer because of their pride." Job 35:12

Being prideful in other ways is what keeps us distant from others as well. We sometimes don't reach out to others for help because our pride keeps us from wanting to look as though we need any help at all. We like to appear as though we have it all together when in reality, we may not.

Social media feeds into this pride in a very clever and undermining way by placating false appearances. Married couples posing for pictures looking happy, but actually fighting every single day. Selfies with filters to make us look better than we actually do, erasing wrinkles, bad skin and altering our least favorite features. Check-ins showing others where we're going and what we're doing especially on special occasions or on trips so our lives appear to be full and happy when in actuality, we could be very depressed or so lost in life and purpose that no vacation could ever fill the voids we carry.

The enemy loves this and he loves working through people through social media because it's a very sneaky way for him to create division, as well as, insecurity and negative thoughts.

So do not compare yourself to what you see on people's social media pages. Unfollow those who should no longer be part of your life. Stop posting private things about your life. Save those revealing pictures for your spouse only. And do not covet (desire or be jealous for) others or what they appear to be or have based on what they post on social media. Do not give the enemy a foothold in your life.

> **"At one time, I lived without understanding the law. But when I learned the command not to covet, for instance, the power of sin came to life, and I died. So I discovered that the law's commands, which were supposed to bring life, brought spiritual death instead." Romans 7:9-10**

There is no relationship that can escape the wrath of the enemy if God's commands are not be adhered to by all those involved. The enemy can cause strife in marriages, in familial bonds, in friendships and in workplace relations. He will do this in every area of your life if you allow him to.

Fight against his pathetic strategies to cause division in your relationships by discerning his tactics and understanding that he talks through weak and wounded people to cause anger, unforgiveness and pride to take root in our hearts.

But God is bigger and stronger. You serve a BIG God. He can change the hearts and minds of anyone hardened against us to save a marriage, strengthen a family bond, repair a broken friendship and even reestablish good working relations in the workplace. He can affect anyone and anything because He created it ALL. He can change the mind and heart of whomever He wills.

Look at Pharaoh the King of Egypt, for example. God caused him to free the Israelites after 40 years of enslavement that greatly benefited the Egyptians. Pharaoh was the most important and powerful person in the Egyptian kingdom. He was the head of the government and the high priest of every temple.

The Pharaoh was so highly positioned that the Egyptians considered him half-man, half-god. The Pharaoh owned all of Egypt. So no one could make him do anything he didn't want to do much less anything that would benefit his kingdom less such as freeing slaves.

So why on earth would Pharaoh agree to free the Israelites when they worked under his command, building and serving his kingdom without wages? Why would he care that Moses wanted the Israelites to be able to serve God when Pharaoh considered himself a god? Why? Because it was God's Will and desire for him to. God's changed the Pharaoh's mind and heart.

> **"Pharaoh sent for Moses and Aaron during the night, 'Get out!' he ordered. Leave my people – and take the rest of the Israelites with you! Go and worship the Lord as you have requested." Exodus 12:31**

God can download ideas into our minds to serve His own purpose anytime He wants to. Unfortunately, the enemy can too. So there's a spiritual battle of tug-o-war for our thoughts going on each and every day. We must learn to discern which ideas and strategies are from God and which ones are not.

If your spouse has told you she is leaving you, or your child has chosen a path leading away from God, understand that their actions might possibly be influenced by evil thoughts from the enemy that they think are their own. Declare this scripture over them daily and watch God move in their lives:

> **"And I will give you a new heart, and I will put a new spirit in you. I will take out your stony, stubborn heart and give you a tender, responsive heart. And I will put my Spirit in you so that you will follow my decrees and be careful to obey my regulations." Ezekiel 36:26-27**

Believe me, God hears your prayers and He can change anyone's mind and heart. After all, if He caused Paul to believe in his heart and mind that Jesus Christ was the Messiah sent from God and to write the majority of the New Testament after he was actually murdering Christians with those same beliefs, He can certainly change your spouse's or child's mind and heart.

God heals. He repairs brokenness. He restores wholeness, and He also transforms hearts and minds.

CHAPTER ELEVEN
"Death and Life of Ideas or Strategies"

Is it possible that our minds could be drafted into battles and wars without us even realizing it?

In the military, strategies are considered to be active plans over movements and operations during a war or battle. Outwitting the enemy is the way to win a war. To be one step ahead. To show up unexpectedly and attack the enemy while keeping yourself surrounded with allies and an armor of protection.

The same is true for a battle of the mind.

Whether or not you realize it, there is a daily war going on in your mind between your own thoughts and those thoughts the enemy puts in your mind and tries to disguise as your own.

> **"Those who are dominated by the sinful nature think about sinful things, but those who are controlled by the Holy Spirit think about things that please the Holy Spirit." Romans 8:5**

Negative, self-deprecating, self-crucifying thoughts are not yours – they're the enemy's. His thoughts will lead you down wrong paths. He doesn't want you to carry out your divine destiny or live abundantly. He wants the divine ideas and strategies that God gives you to wither and die before they take root in your life.

> **"So letting your sinful nature control your mind leads to death. But letting the Spirit control your mind leads to life and peace. For sinful nature is always hostile to God. It never did obey God's laws, And it never will."**
> **Romans 8:6-7**

God has not created you to live in darkness. Not even in your mind. He has created you in His own image. So what is in Him, is in you, as well.

> **"God is light, and there is no darkness in Him at all."**
> **1 John 1:5**

In God and in you, there is no condemnation or bondage. There is encouragement and freedom. There is the building up of your self image. Daily reminders of your talents and gifts flow through your mind. God gives birth to new ideas and plans for you. He downloads them to you from the Holy Spirit.

> **"For I know the plans I have for you, says the Lord. They are plans for good and not for disaster, to give you a future and a hope." Jeremiah 29:11**

God will send you strategies to outwit the enemy and give you a divine "edge". Let's say, you're hoping to get a promotion and you're up against other co-workers each vying for the same position. God can download fresh, new, never-heard-of ideas to you in order to impress your boss and give you the "edge" over your co-workers.

He can also cause your boss to be divinely impressed with your ideas and offer the promotion to you. He will do this when He knows that you will use your promotional position and/or the increase in finances to bless others and not just to live a better life for yourself.

"For God will put a plan into their minds, a plan the will carry out His purposes." Proverbs 17:17

God's ideas will prosper you in the Kingdom of God giving rise to new opportunities for you to spread the Gospel of Jesus Christ. He may place an opportunity in front of you to bless others using the gifts He put inside of you. Then He will bless you right back with a huge bonus or supernatural financial increase.

"The Lord will send rain at the proper time from His rich treasury in the heavens and will bless all the work you do. You will lend to many nations but you will never need to borrow from them." Deuteronomy 28:12

When He does this for you, it will be something that no man can stop or interfere with as long as you are obedient to Him.

"I know all the things you do, And I have opened a door for you that no one can close. You have little strength yet you obeyed my Word and did not deny me." Revelation 3:8

The enemy's ideas will prosper you in such a way as to distance you from blessing others. He will tempt you with monetary gain for purely selfish reasons that will benefit only you, while causing harm to others.

For example, he may place an opportunity in your path that would result in a huge raise but require late night meetings/parties with potential clients to land business deals. The increase in salary would be enough to pay off your debt, buy a house and add some excitement to your life. However the overtime, increased number of hours and late nightlife would negatively affect your family long-term, possibly even resulting in divorce and estrangement from your children.

"When you follow the desires of your sinful nature, the results are very clear: sexual immorality, impurity, quarreling, jealously, outbursts of anger, selfish

ambition, dissention, division, envy, drunkenness, wild parties and other sins like these. Let me tell you again, as I have before, that anyone living like that will not inherit the Kingdom of God." Galatians 5:19-21

The ideas given to you by God will ensure your happiness here on earth as well as your eternal destiny in heaven. The ideas given to you by the enemy will ensure your demise here on earth and keep you out of the Kingdom of God for eternity which is, of course, his goal.

So, if you're looking for godly ideas and strategies to come to you, you must speak life in to them. Remember that your words have life-giving power.

You can't speak negatively and expect new ideas to enter your mind. For example, you can't say things like, "I'm never going to figure out a way to get out of all this debt and buy a house."

If you do this, you're cursing yourself and crushing your chances to get what you desire.

Allow Jesus to guide you along your path, and that path will lead you straight to legacy-level blessings and destiny.

CHAPTER TWELVE

"Death and Life of Dreams, Promises or Destiny"

*Have you noticed that some believers step right
in to their God-ordained destiny while others
remain struggling for the rest of their lives?*

God is progressive, always moving forward and never looking back. He does not live in the past. He does not condemn, He does not change His mind nor does He go back on His Word. God is peace, light and order.

"God is not a God of disorder but of peace, as in all the meetings of God's holy people." 1 Corinthians 14:33

In order to access all that God has for us, we must be these things too.

We must never get caught up in a lazy slumber succumbing to a cycle of unproductiveness. This can open the door to the enemy and lead to a downward spiral of depression. God has created us to be intelligent, able, creative beings. He has set us high above every other creature He has created.

"If you listen to the commands of the Lord your God that I am giving you today, and if you carefully obey them, the Lord will make you the head and not the tail, and you must always be at the top and never at the bottom." Deuteronomy 28:13

We must not define ourselves by our past mistakes or bad decisions. We must forgive ourselves just as we have been commanded by God to forgive others and move forward toward new patterns and new behaviors that are aligned with God's Will for our lives.

We must never condemn ourselves for being human and falling short of God's Will. We will sin because we have a sinful nature that was brought to us from Adam.

> **"Yes, Adam's one sin brings condemnation for everyone, but Christ's one act of righteousness brings a right relationship with God and new life for everyone."**
> **Romans 5:18**

So, when we sin, we must repent and make changes in our thoughts, behaviors and words to align ourselves with Jesus Christ. God will help us to do this when we earnestly seek His help and repent with true sincerity.

> **"Don't copy the behavior and customs of this world, but let God transform you into a new person by changing the way you think. Then you will learn to know God's Will for you, which is good and pleasing and perfect." Romans 12:2**

Because our thoughts control our words, we must think about ourselves the way Jesus does and speak life into our future dreams, promises and destiny in order to see them manifest in our lives.

But only if our dreams are aligned with God's plans for our lives and we are obedient to Him in all our ways, we will see them come to fruition. God's plan for us is what will be, not our own desires.

If we follow our own desires utilizing the free will God has given each of us, then we will have brought death to the dreams, promises and destiny that God had ordained for us before we were even born. Maybe we will see some success in our endeavors by ignoring God's plans and seeking our own man-made destiny, but this success will unknowingly align us with the enemy, not with God.

We have each been born with a divine purpose. And in order to access it, we must humble ourselves before God, submitting our will to His. God's destiny for us far exceeds anything that man-made plans could ever achieve. It's a very distinctive difference. God's destiny for our lives will always involve blessing and loving others and incorporating all of God's commands in our daily living.

> **"Bring all the tithes into the storehouse so there will be enough food in my temple. 'If you do', says the Lord, 'I will open the windows of heaven for you. I will pour out a blessing so great, you won't have enough room to take it in! Try it! Put me to the test! Your crops will be abundant, for I will guard them from insects and disease. Your grapes will not fall from the vine before they are ripe', says the Lord of heavens armies. Then all nations will call you blessed, for your land will be such a delight." Malachi 3:10-12**

This means that God's plan is to make you prominent and wealthy if you bless others, sow seeds and tithe a portion what He has given to you in honor to Him. You must acknowledge that He is your source, not this world. His plan is to guard and protect all of your endeavors, investments and finances, and to ensure your success. He will guide you.

We are created to be wealthy, successful, prominent and happy. Jesus came to increase us in every possible area of our lives and deliver us from every demonic principality that would keep us from His plan for our lives.

> **"The thief's purpose is to steal and kill and destroy. My purpose is to give them a rich and satisfying life." John 10:10**

We must speak these scriptures over our lives with a faith that cannot be shaken, in order to see them take root and come to life.

CHAPTER THIRTEEN
"Developing Unshakeable Faith"

*How many of us have faith in God's power
and abilities but as soon as we're in the
middle of an overwhelming circumstance,
we get nervous, concerned or worried about
what will happen next?*

That place of wavering faith, uncertainty and doubt is exactly where the enemy wants you to be because in that place is where your miracles, breakthroughs and prayers are blocked.

"If you need wisdom, ask our generous God, and He will give it to you. He will not rebuke you for asking. But when you ask Him be sure that your faith is in God alone. Do not waver, for a person with divided loyalty is as unsettled as a wave of the sea that is blown and tossed by the wind. Such people should not expect to receive anything from the Lord. Their loyalty is divided between God and the world, and they are unstable in everything they do." James 1:5-8

Do not let this happen.

Do not allow the enemy to steal what's rightfully yours.

You must understand that when your faith is not firmly rooted in your spirit, it is weak and can be shaken. This instability makes you vulnerable to the struggles of this world. The enemy will use this to trap you in to sin and get you to unknowingly partner up with the world. Partnering with the world makes you an enemy of God.

> **"You adulterers! Don't you realize that friendship with the world makes you an enemy of God? I say it again: If you want to be a friend of the world, you make yourself an enemy of God." James 4:4**

This is serious stuff!

Most of us don't realize that getting nervous about how we're going to pay our bills or about what the doctor's report says is an action that puts us in an adversarial position against God.

This may come as a surprise to many of us, but it shouldn't because God's Word is truth. It's the only truth. In it, He says we are whole and healed and provided for by Him.

We have to make the choice to either believe His word and promises to us or not to believe them. There is no grey area in this. It's one way or the other. It's the world's truth or its not.

It is His command that we trust in Him, believe in Him and obey Him. If we do not do this, then we love the world, not God.

> **"If you love me, obey my commands." John 14:15**

> **"There is no judgment in anyone who believes in Him. But anyone who does not believe in Him has already been judged for not believing in God's one and only Son." John 3:18**

Believing in God's one and only Son, Jesus Christ, is not just knowing who He is and what He did. Even the enemy and all of his demon followers know and believe that. But rather, believing in Him means that you believe in his power, His superiority and His supreme authority over everything living and non-living.

Wavering faith angers God.

> **"And anyone who believes in God's Son has eternal life. Anyone who doesn't obey the Son will never experience eternal life but remains under God's angry judgment." John 3:36**

Wavering faith proves to Him that you are not His because those who truly believe in Him and follow Him, know Him and know His ability to heal and provide. So they do not waver in their faith.

> **"I am the good Sheppard: I know my own sheep, and they know me, just as my Father knows me and I know the Father. So I sacrifice my life for the sheep." John 10:14-15**

Momentary wavering is something God understands in the midst of a sudden break of bad news. We are human, after all. But He expects us to have the self-control to not allow our emotions to overtake us, and instead to allow our spirit to lead. We are expected to bring our concerns to Him and give them to Him with faith and trust and belief so He can work on our behalf.

> **"Give all your worries and cares to God, for He cares about you. Stay alert! Watch out for your great enemy, the devil. He prowls around like a roaring lion, looking for someone to devour. Stand firm in your faith. Remember that your family of believers all over the world is going through the same kind of suffering you are.**
>
> **In His kindness God called you to share in His eternal glory by means of Christ Jesus. So after you**

have suffered a little while, He will restore, support, and strengthen you and He will place you on a firm foundation. All power to Him Forever! Amen."
1 Peter 5:7-11

You see, when you bring your concerns to God, He will fix whatever needs fixing, healing whatever illness the doctor says you have and provide you with all of the resources you need. He won't stop there either. He guarantees to place you on a firm foundation as well. This means that He will make sure you are ready for the blessings you've received so that you won't falter or struggle in that place.

He is a good, loving, caring daddy. You are the object of His affection. You are the absolute apple of His eye. He adores you and wants you to be established, financially secure, healthy, fully-physically functional and stable in all your ways.

If you seek His help and stay focused on Him rather than your problem, He will cause your faith to be developed.

> **"We do this by keeping our eyes on Jesus, the champion who initiates and perfects our faith." Hebrews 12:2**

Faith that cannot be shaken is initially found by learning and knowing the Word of God.

> **"So then faith cometh by hearing and hearing by the Word of God." Romans 10:17**

After spending enough time in the Word and becoming familiar with it, you will mature spiritually. You will begin to experience God's workings in your life as your problems get taken care of on a supernatural level that is unexplainable in any natural way. You will see His favor and blessings working miracles in your life and the words you read in the bible will suddenly come to life and gain power in your heart.

This begins to build and strengthen your faith.

Reinforcement of an even deeper faith built on the foundation you already have at this time comes from then listening to others speak about their faith and what their faith has shown them. In other words, as you hear testimonies of the blessings, healings and restoration God has given to others through faith, an unwavering faith will actually take up permanent residence in your heart.

It will become a "worry blocker" against future circumstances. Your faith will be unshakeable and your favor and blessings will overflow.

When you have your "worry blocking" wall built up in your mind, heart and spirit, nothing can penetrate it. You will handle difficult circumstances with a newfound strength and fortitude.

You will feel stronger, better and more capable than ever before because you know beyond a shadow of any doubt that God "has your back". He lives in you. He is part of you. He will protect you against all harm every minute of every day, and you know it.

> **"God dwells in that city; it cannot be destroyed. From the very break of day, God will protect it." Psalms 46:5**
>
> **"For the Lord protects the bones of the righteous; not one of them is broken." Psalms 34:20**
>
> **"The Lord protects all those who love Him but He destroys the wicked." Psalms 145:20**

He will protect your mind, your heart, your body and your spirit. There is nothing He will not protect you against whether it is seen or unseen.

Most of us aren't even aware that the angels assigned to us are fighting daily battles in the spirit and protecting us from demonic attack. We can't see them, but they're there.

"For He will order His angels to protect you wherever you go." Psalms 91:11

They are warriors, fighting on our behalf against demonic attacks. We must grow strongly enough in our faith to become warriors too.

CHAPTER FOURTEEN
"Becoming a Warrior"

*Did you know that God specifically
designed and equipped you for battle
before you were even born?*

The battle you fight is one you are grafted in to by association with Jesus Christ. Being a creation of God, you are automatically loathed, hunted and pursued by the enemy. He hates you passionately. He even hates innocent babies and children. In fact, the very second you are conceived, he begins his battle against you.

He may try to take you out in your mother's womb, causing a miscarriage. He may try to injure your neonatal development in some way causing signs of disability and put suggestions of abortion in the mouths of doctors to try to convince your parents to end your life themselves.

He will suggest to them through professionals that the quality of life their child will have is so poor that it would actually be cruel for them to not abort the baby. He will play with the minds of everyone involved and stop at nothing, in order to keep that life from being born.

He knows when you've been conceived and he immediately begins waiting and watching for the moment he can strike his first attack against you.

The enemy is violently angry and delusionally insane. He is like a spoiled child who won't stop until he gets his way, stomping his feet and screaming and throwing tantrums. He doesn't care who you are, how old you are or what you look like. He opposes anyone who is a creation of God.

His battles against all of God's children are non-stop, never-ending and merciless. They are all part of the war that exists between the enemy and God.

The war began the moment Lucifer, the once cherished archangel of God, was permanently thrown out of heaven by God.

> **"Yes," he told them, "I saw satan fall from heaven like lightening!" Luke 10:18**

Lucifer, the enemy known as satan, was created as an anointed cherub by God and given the position of captain of the cherub hosts. He was the angel of creativity which is why you see his evil, demonic influences in movies, music and video games.

Sometime prior to the creation of natural order, satan became vain and prideful of his position and beauty. He irrationally sought the authority of God over the universe for himself and desired to far surpass God's glory and actually take His place as ruler over the universe.

He also desired to have authority over other archangels, Michael and Gabriel, as well as all the angels they ruled over. He became rebellious against God and wanted to overthrow him to gain God's position and take his place in the third heaven.

> **"I was caught up to the third Heaven ..."
> 2 Corinthians 12:2**

There are three levels of heaven. The third heaven, also called Paradise, is where God lives. The second heaven is where the angles reside. This is stellar heaven which is amongst the stars and beyond the earth's atmosphere. The first heaven is the sky, the atmosphere of the earth.

Satan was permanently cast out of third heaven along with the one-third of angels that were under his authority, who are now the demons submitted to and working for satan. He is able to travel between second and first heaven, but he isn't permitted to enter third heaven ever again. For him, there is no redemption. No second chance. He will never again be in the direct presence of God.

But you will, and the enemy hates this about you.

Through Christ, you have the ability to be saved and reside with God for eternity. This enrages the enemy. He didn't get a second chance. He was kicked out of heaven without forgiveness. He's so jealous of you for that and for being demoted to a level below you that he's insanely vengeful. He will stop at nothing to get as many of God's children to be permanently kicked out of heaven along with him as he possibly can as a punishment to God who loves and adores you.

It's kind of a "misery loves company" type of situation. It's also a "you hurt me, so I'm going to hurt you worse" mentality. The enemy knows where he's going to end up. He knows scripture. He knows he loses in the end, but that doesn't slow him down. In fact, it fuels his desire to take as many people with him as possible.

So his battle against you begins the very second you are conceived, before you have even taken your first breath. He doesn't even want you to be born. He doesn't want you to grow up, learn the truth and influence others to follow Christ. He is trying to control the size of the Lord's army.

When you do make it through the gestational period and you are born, he works tirelessly every day for the rest of your life to adopt you as his follower. He stops at nothing to influence your mind to think evil thoughts.

> **"This is what the Sovereign Lord says: at that time evil thoughts will come to your mind, and you will devise a wicked scheme." Ezekiel 38:10**

He wants to keep you from learning the truth and following the commands of God. He knows when you follow God's commands, you will be able to circumvent his traps, setups and plans, and you will be positioned to spend eternity with God.

So the battles you fight throughout your lifetime are for the salvation of your soul and for the salvation of as many other people's souls as possible.

We all fight our own different battles in the same exact war.

Some of these battles are emotional like betrayal, heartache, depression, insecurity, or anger over situations that are out of our control.

Others are financial or business related wherein income flow has become suddenly blocked or hindered.

The presence of illness and disease are also physical manifestations of spiritual battles; and abuse can be both a physical and emotional battle experienced at the same time.

Make absolutely no mistake about it, you were designed and born to fight! You were created to be a warrior in Christ. God has placed everything inside of you that you need to fight and to win.

He is waiting for you to tap into the power He has given you through Jesus Christ, and press through the difficulties in your life so you can be used by Him to save the souls of others.

Your battles teach you, stretch you, prepare you and transform you into a warrior for Christ. This is why He allows them to happen. It's tough love. It's the only way we learn to fight. If everything went perfectly for us all the time, what reason would there be to change or grow?

A supernatural process of transformation comes from fighting our own battles and gaining higher levels of faith. Each struggle brings us one step closer to whom God created us to be.

Your life is a basic training program for warring against what you can't see with your eyes but what you can see manifesting in your life in the natural.

So how do you win these battles?

The first step to wining the battles in your life and becoming the warrior you were created to be is to understand exactly WHAT you're fighting against.

> **"For we are not fighting against flesh and blood enemies, but against evil rulers and authorities of the unseen world, against mighty powers in this dark world, and against evil spirits in the heavenly places."**
> **Ephesians 6:12**

The enemy works through weak and wounded people. Even your friends and family are used by the enemy to trap you in to sin. The enemy will speak through your loved ones because he knows you will listen to what they have to say. He knows you trust them and value their opinion.

For example, he may use your friends to convince you to get a job and drop out of school in order to distance you from your destiny. He will speak through them to tell you that you could be making money and going out with them instead of studying all the time. He will cause them to say that college degrees don't guarantee jobs or a certain level of money, and that you should stop wasting your time going to school. He may also cause them to convince you that paying off school debt will monopolize your money, so you should just start working now and saving up for your future.

Because you trust their opinions, you may be inclined to listen to their advice, not realizing that their advice is actually coming straight from hell.

He may use your family to cause a fight with you by putting thoughts in their head to cause them to say things he knows will upset you. He does this because he wants you to be angry at each other and argue. This of course gives him a foothold in your life and something to accuse you about with God in the heavenly court.

It also causes division which the enemy loves because it isolates you, rendering you weaker and much more vulnerable to his setups.

So do as God says and use discernment when you're given advice. Go to God and ask Him what He wants you to do. He's the boss. He's the one directing you toward your destiny. Never allow the enemy to direct you away from it or delay the things God has for you.

Let your spirit lead rather than your flesh. Do not succumb to the tricks of the enemy.

> **"And 'don't sin by letting anger control you."**
> **Ephesians 4:26**
>
> **"Human anger does not produce the righteousness God desires." James 1:20**

The next step to winning the battles in your life and becoming a warrior, after understanding what you're fighting against, is to learn HOW to fight.

How do the military fight? They armor up in their fighting gear, they use weapons of destruction and they follow the commands of their superiors who have a plan of attack laid out for them to follow, leading them to victory.

Military armor generally consists of protective head, chest and foot gear. In biblical times, men wore a metal helmet, sandals with iron studs on the leather soles, a metal breastplate that was held up with a leather metal-studded belt, and a shield. Each piece of their armor was significant and necessary for protecting something very specific. In order to be victorious in fighting their enemies, soldiers needed this protective armor because they didn't always know what weapon would be used against them. They needed to be prepared for every type of warfare that could possibly be used.

The same is true for each one of us.

We need to be armored up and well-protected for war against the enemy. We don't always know what kind of weapons will form against us, so God has described specific pieces of spiritual armor that if worn together, will earn victory against the enemy every single time.

In the book of Ephesians, God compares the physical pieces of armor worn by soldiers to the spiritual armor we need to have in order to successfully fight our enemy, satan.

> **"Therefore, put on every piece of God's armor so you will be able to resist the enemy in the time of evil. Then after the battle you will still be standing firm." Ephesians 6:13**

A belt worn by a biblical soldier held up a very heavy breastplate designed to protect his heart against piercing wounds. Without the belt, the heavy breastplate couldn't be supported. In God's comparison to our spiritual warfare, He calls this belt of truth, and He calls the breastplate the body armor of righteousness.

> **"Stand your ground putting on the body armor of God's righteousness." Ephesians 6:14**

What God is trying to get us to understand with this analogy is that just as the belt is necessary to keep the breastplate on, being truthful is necessary in order to live righteously. These 2 virtues are the most important means of defense against the enemy's attacks. This is why God lists them first. They give us the power we need to activate the protection of the Lord's army of angels.

In other words, when we live in righteousness and honesty, the angels that have been assigned to us are ordered by God and divinely activated to do their jobs and fight our battles in the spiritual realm against evil principalities. Many of these battles take place without our knowledge.

God then continues his analogy by comparing the soldier's shoes to God's peace which is another very significant weapon against the enemy.

"For shoes, put on the peace that comes from the Good News so that you will be fully prepared."
Ephesians 6:15

The shoes they wore had metal studs on the bottom of the soles to aid in traction for climbing tough terrain and mountains. These special shoes allowed the soldiers to keep moving forward, toward their destinations, without stopping, despite the terrain they were up against.

For us, this means that by wearing the peace of God, or having His peace deeply rooted within us like the studs were rooted in the shoes, we will be able to keep moving forward toward our purpose and destiny no matter what the enemy decides to throw against us. The size and incline of any mountain put in our path will not stop us from reaching our destiny.

Another piece of armory used by soldiers was a shield. They were huge, heavy pieces of metal that were held up to deflect arrows that their enemies shot at them. These shields were completely impenetrable by arrows. Arrows would bounce right off them even though they were intended to kill the soldiers.

Like the soldiers, God has given us a shield to protect ourselves with when the enemy attacks us. Our impenetrable shield is faith.

"In addition to all of these, hold up the shield of faith to stop the fiery arrows of the devil." Ephesians 6:16

Faith is very powerful. It is just as protective as a thick, metal, impenetrable shield. When we have unshakeable faith, we have an untouchable strength that nothing can come even close to destroying. With faith, the attacks, or arrows of the enemy, bounce right off of us.

Faith moves God to activate supernatural properties to override natural ones. This is when miracles happen. Nothing can stop the power of faith in your life no matter what the circumstance is, including the enemy.

So what does he do? He targets your mind. If he can put thoughts of doubt in your mind to weaken your faith, then he'll literally win every single spiritual battle that you're engaged in. He'll be able to steal your destiny as well as your salvation.

This is why God commands you to:

"Put on salvation as your helmet..." Ephesians 6:17

Helmets protected soldier's heads during the battle. An unprotected head would lead to death. That held true during biblical warfare and it holds true for you today, during spiritual battles. An unprotected mind will lead to the spiritual death of your soul because your thoughts can preclude your salvation. Salvation is the deliverance from sin and its consequences, and it all begins in the mind and what you believe.

Believing anything except biblical truth will cost you your salvation. The enemies knows this. His ultimate goal is to destroy your salvation so he can take your soul to hell with him when he goes and separate you from God for eternity. So he tells you lies in hopes you'll take the bait and believe them. He'll do it in such a way that you might begin to believe that his thoughts are actually your own. He's very cunning and tricky. He is the father of lies. That's all the he does is lie.

> **"He has always hated the truth, because there is no truth in him. When he lies, it is consistent with his character; for he is a liar and the father of lies." John 8:44**

The reason he hates truth is because that's what sets you free and saves your soul.

"And you will know the truth, and the truth will set you free." John 8:32

Untruth will cause you to do and say things that are against the commands of God, thus leading to your spiritual death. Your mind determines the words you speak and the actions you carry out. So this is the very first thing the enemy will attack. If the enemy can get you to believe the evil thoughts and lies that he puts in your mind, then he can essentially cause you to destroy our own salvation with our words and behavior. This is why God tells us how imperative it is that we protect our minds.

Not only can you destroy our own salvation, but you can block God's favor and destiny on your life by not protecting your thoughts. For example, let's say the enemy puts the thought in your mind that you are never going to buy a house. He tells you that you don't make enough money and never will, and that you're not worthy of owning a home.

If you believe this, you will start speaking life into it. You'll say things to your friends like, "I'm never going to get out of this apartment. I'll never be able to afford a house." These are words spoken over your life and are actually word curses that can block financial blessings from being released into your life.

Believing those lies about yourself may also cause you to spend money unwisely rather than saving it because it would seem useless to try to save for something that you believe is so far beyond what you can afford. This lack of faith in God's abundant provision will block you from receiving God's supernatural favor.

On the other hand, if you didn't believe the enemy's lies and instead believed what God says in the Word, you'd begin putting money aside for a future purchase as an act of good faith in your belief, and you'd speak life into the bright future you have in Christ Jesus. As a result, this good measure act of faith would manifest into God's supernatural favor in your life and you'd someday realize your dreams.

Rejecting the enemy's untruthful thoughts as your own requires spiritual discernment and discipline. This can only be done by protecting our thoughts at all times with a "helmet of salvation".

The last, but undoubtedly most powerful, weapon in the artillery of the biblical soldier was their sword. Made of metal and sharpened by stones to the point of an extremely fine point, their sword could easily cut through any resistant garment or hard structure, including the human head. The sword was the only offensive weapon in their artillery. All of the other weapons were designed to defend and protect the soldier, but the sword could actually kill the enemy.

God calls His Word a sword and commands us to use it as a very powerful weapon against the enemy in much the same way the biblical soldiers used theirs.

> **"... and take the sword of the Spirit, which is the Word of God." Ephesians 6:17**

The Word of God is the most resistant and formidable weapon in existence. Nothing and no one can destroy its power! It is a LIVING weapon which makes it unlike any other weapon that has ever existed. It is active and able to kill the enemies and attacks of the spiritual world as well as those manifesting in the natural one.

> **"For the Word of God is alive and powerful. It is sharper than the sharpest two-edged sword, cutting between soul and spirit, between joint and marrow. It exposes our innermost thoughts and desires." Hebrews 4:12**

Decreeing and declaring the Word of God as a weapon is the best way to "kill" the enemy's attacks against you. In fact, that's exactly what Jesus did to fight satan in the desert. This was His example to us as to how extremely powerful of a weapon the Word is.

"Then Jesus was led by the Spirit into the wilderness to be tempted there by the devil. For forty days and forty nights He fasted and became very hungry.

During that time the devil came and said to Him, If you are the Son of God, tell these stones to become loaves of bread.'

(It is when we are weak and vulnerable that the enemy comes to tempt us just as he did with Jesus. The enemy will question who we are, even though he knows our destiny and capabilities through Jesus. He will try to get us to bow to him by doubting whom God has created us to be)
But Jesus told him,

"No! The Scriptures say, 'People do not live by bread alone, but by every word that comes from the mouth of God."

(Jesus fought back with Scripture. That was His weapon)

Then the devil took Him to the holy city, Jerusalem, to the highest point of the Temple, and said,

'If you are the Son of God, jump off! For the Scriptures say, 'He will order His angels to protect you. And they will hold you up with their hands so you won't even hurt your foot on a stone.'

(Once again, satan undermines Jesus by saying "If you are the Son of God..." Satan knows who Jesus is and he knows His power. If he did this to Jesus, he will do the exact same thing to you. He will try to get you to doubt yourself or get you to think lower of yourself in order to put you in a vulnerable state of mind)

(Also, notice that satan quotes Scripture quite well. He knows Scripture, so he knows when you don't adhere to it. This is very important to realize)

Jesus responded,

"The Scriptures also say, 'You must not test the Lord your God.'

Next the devil took Him to the peak of a very high mountain and showed Him all the kingdoms of the world and their glory.

'I will give it all to you, he said, 'if you would kneel down and worship me.'

(Notice the persistence of the enemy. This is the third time he is attempting to revert Jesus away from His God-ordained destiny. The enemy will do the exact same thing to you. He is relentless and persistent. Expect this)

He offers Jesus all the kingdoms on earth. This is because all of the kingdoms that were once given to Adam, became satan's when Adam sinned. The enemy is the king of this world and can give riches to those who bow to him. So when you see someone living well, understand that their wealth and success isn't necessarily from God)

'Get out of here, satan', Jesus told him.
'For the Scriptures say, You must worship the Lord your God and serve Him only'

(Take note of how Jesus not only quoted Scripture again as a weapon but also commanded satan to leave him alone. You must do this too. You must realize that you have the power to command the enemy just as Jesus did because Jesus resides within you and works through you)

When the devil had finished tempting Jesus, he left him until the next opportunity came, and angels came and took care of Jesus." Matthew 4:1-11

Jesus used the Word of God as a weapon, and the enemy left Him. The attack was stopped. This is our example of what we need to do: Decree and declare the Word of God over ourselves and our situation while wearing the rest of God's armor. This is how we win the battles in our lives that are meant to keep us from God's best.

Adhering to the word of God also means that we are following the commands of our Superior (God). Superiors of an army lay out the plan of attack against their enemy for their soldiers and lead them to victory.

The plan of attack against satan is wearing the armor of God and following His commands. Our obedience and submission to God's Will is how we fight to win against the enemy and become the warriors that we were created to be.

However, we must be aware that the enemy knows when we believe what we are decreeing and declaring versus merely reading words on a page. So we must believe in our hearts, minds and spirits that our armor is enough to win battles against the enemy.

The enemy can "smell" fear and unbelief. Although he cannot create anything at all like God can, he does have some supernatural power and ability because he was a former anointed cherub of God's.

So you must become strong in spirit and overcome all fear of the enemy in order to successfully fight against his attacks on your life and your destiny.

CHAPTER FIFTEEN

"Overcoming Fear of the Enemy"

Even if you're properly armed, you can't
effectively fight what you fear, right?

Most single women don't want a gun in their home because they think they may be too scared to use it. Their biggest concern is: What if someone breaks in to their home and the gun is taken away from them by the intruder and used on them?

In this scenario, the woman's fear would be sensed by the intruder who'd render her weapon useless and then use it to kill her instead of the other way around. This scenario has actually become a reality for many people in that moment of sudden surprise and panic.

The same thing can happen with the enemy.

If you tell him to get out of your house or out of your situation but you're scared of him, he will know it. In fact, he may even use your fear against you by intimidating you even more in the future to discourage you from gaining the courage to successfully rebuke him.

Remember that he was once an anointed cherub. So even though his power is not at all equal to that of Jesus, he does have some supernatural abilities. He can put thoughts in your mind. He can affect the weather. He can affect things in the air like electricity, radio waves, internet, and sound waves. He can even disguise himself as an angel.

"But I am not surprised! Even satan disguises himself as an angel of light." 2 Corinthians 11:14

The enemy's minion workers can do these things too. They can appear as ghosts and terrorize people. In fact, movies often depict demons as being more powerful than us. This is a farce. It's a lie straight from the pit of hell. In reality, the enemy and his deranged minions are below our feet and under our dominion.

"He subdues the nations before us, putting our enemies beneath our feet." Psalms 47:3

Believing the lie that the enemy and his minions are more powerful than you are can block your blessings, diminish your ability to fight the enemy and create doubt in your own ability since you were created in God's image.

This angers God. Don't fall prey to these lies. The enemy is below you and can only scare you if you allow him to.

What the enemy CAN do is "feel" your faith. If you're decreeing the Word of God but you don't believe what you're saying or that it has imminent power against him, then he will be laughing at you as you're reciting it.

So before you begin using the Word of God as the weapon that it is, be sure to grasp the following things:

You have been created in the image of God and given all power through Jesus Christ.

God has given you the most powerful armory in existence.

God has given you dominion over everything seen and unseen.

Even the angels assigned to you are under your dominion. You have angels assigned to you that never leave your side.

> **"For He will order His angels to protect you wherever you go." Psalms 91:11**

They are not human. They are angelic creatures that are formidable and intimidatingly strong. They are huge. They aren't cute little spiritual beings with little wings as you might see in a picture or molded into a statue. Angels in a completely different class are like that, but the warrior angels are like giants with supernatural strength. They are a force to be reckoned with. Their entire purpose is to fight and protect. They were designed and created specifically to be warrior members of Jesus Christ's army.

> **"The Lord of Heaven's Armies is here among us; the God of Israel is our fortress." Psalms 46:7**

The archangel Michael leads this spiritual military stronghold, Heaven's Armies. So you are never alone. You are joined in your fight by angels assigned to your protection and by God Himself. He has promised you that you will win all battles when you are obedient to Him in all your ways.

> **"No weapon formed against you will prosper." Isaiah 54:17**

> **"The Lord will conquer your enemies when they attack you. They will attack you from one direction, but they will scatter from you in seven." Deuteronomy 28:7**

Obedience will unlock supernatural doors for you. God will create a boldness in you that you never thought you'd ever have. There will be no natural explanation for it.

Knowing that you're not fighting alone, you will need to begin to rebuke the enemy from your situations, from your finances, from you relationships and from your mind.

Here's an example of what you can say out loud, "Those thoughts are not mine and I rebuke them in the name of Jesus Christ." Then quote scriptures like those listed above, Isaiah 54:17 and Deuteronomy 28:7.

In doing this, you'll notice things changing in the atmosphere around you. You'll feel Christ's power working through you. This will gradually build you up even more until one day, you'll realize the fear you once had is gone.

You'll understand that the big, scary devil depicted in movies is actually not big and scary at all. He's a psychotic wannabe who is rendered completely powerless by the power of Jesus Christ.

> **"With His own blood – not the blood of goats and calves – He entered the Most Holy Place once for all time and secured our redemption forever." Hebrews 9:12**

Plead the blood of Jesus Christ over your and over your situation. His blood is superior to everything and everyone. When Jesus died on that cross, He changed the entire landscape of the enemy's "sin grip" on all of creation. Everything and everyone in heaven, on earth and under earth, must bow and submit to Jesus Christ.

> **"For the Scriptures say, 'As surely as I live,' says the Lord, 'every knee will bend to me, and every tongue will declare allegiance to God." Romans 14:11**

The power of the Word of God is eternal, timeless and never loses its strength. Learning to use the Scriptures for power to win against the enemy will catapult you into abundant living. That's one of the main reasons God provided them for us.

CHAPTER SIXTEEN
"Using Scripture for Power"

*If you're about to engage in battle, do you think
it's enough to know that you have weapons
available to you in your artillery that you haven't
familiarized yourself with, or do you think
you'd need to be familiar with them before using them?*

Understanding your weaponry is even more important than having it in your possession because if you aren't familiar with how to use it, then you won't be able to use it successfully.

Let's say you're being followed by a stranger at night as you're walking to your car in the parking lot of a shopping mall. Maybe you have a can of mace in your purse for just such a situation as this. However, you've never really looked at the can, so you've never realized that there's a safety mechanism on it that must be unlocked in order for it to spray.

The stranger increases his pace toward you. There's no one around to help you. You can feel your heart racing and your breathing deepens. You're scared! You're still no where near your car, but you put your hand in your purse to get your keys out so you can get into your car as quickly as possible and hopefully lock the door before the stranger can get to you. You begin running through the plan in your mind.

Suddenly you feel the can of mace in your purse. You had forgotten that you had it because you've never needed to use it before. You pull it out just in case you don't get into your car before the stranger reaches you.

You can hear the stranger getting closer to you. You realize that you're in serious trouble. You know you won't make it to your car before he gets to you. You know you have to do something fast.

So in a split second, you turn around, hold the can toward his face and push the button. Nothing happens! He grabs you.....

What happened is that you didn't familiarize yourself with the mace can before you needed to use it, so it failed you. It was rendered useless by you. There's absolutely no point in having a weapon available to you that you haven't familiarized yourself with. If you can't actually use the weapon, you might as well not even have it in your possession.

The same is true with your bible. If you're not familiar with it, then it can't help you in your time of need.

On the other hand, if you are familiar with it, the Word of God is a weapon more powerful and effective than any weapon in the natural ever could be.

"For the Word of God will never fail." Luke 1:37

You have to know it and understand it in order to use it. Some people can recite verse after verse of scripture. In fact they know it so well, it's almost like it's a part of them.

How do they do that?

They study the Word daily. They dissect it. They analyze it. They think of the Word as spiritual food to feed their spirit because just as your physical body requires food to thrive and be sustained, so to does your spirit require the spiritual food of the Word of God to thrive and be sustained.

In the book of John, Jesus said,

> **"I live because of the living Father who sent me; in the same way, anyone who feeds on me will live because of me." John 6:57**

So, set aside certain times every day to read the Word and absorb it. Make a schedule and stick to it. You must prioritize the Lord and then He will prioritize you.

> **"Those who obey Him will not be punished. Those who are wise will find a time and a way to do what is right." Ecclesiastes 8:5**

The enemy doesn't want us to know the Word of God. When you don't know your spiritual rights and the laws, it's easy for the enemy to manipulate you in to sin. He loves to make us so busy that we don't have time to read the Word or we're so tired that we make the conscious decision not to do it.

But don't fall for this very common demonic tactic. Never let time control you. Flip that script. You are meant to control time. Time is under your authority just as much as the enemy is. Time is ordered by God to obey you.

If you allow it to control you instead, then you are bowing to it. When you do this, you begin to serve time. It becomes a god in your life, a stronghold, and it will cause chaos and stress in your life.

> **"Be careful at all times to obey the decrees, regulations, instructions and commands that He wrote for you. You must not worship other gods." 2 Kings 17:37**

When you're studying the Word, underline and/or highlight those scriptures in your bible that speak to your situation. Then use these scriptures when you pray. Speak them out, remembering that your words have power in the atmosphere of the spiritual realm.

The Word of God is a living Word. This means that the promises in it are just as active today as they were when they were written down thousands of years ago. If you ask God to direct you to a Word that will help guide you in your current situation, He is faithful to do so. He will cause you to open the bible to the exact place where the answer you're looking for is written.

He wants you to win, not fail. He wants you to progress and advance, not stagnate and get stuck where you are in the midst of struggle.

He has provided to us and for us His Word to use as a powerful medium of spiritual activation. Speaking the Word shifts the atmosphere and activates the angelic presence that surrounds us 24 hours a day, 7 days a week. It's the way the spiritual world works. If you tap into it, you will receive all that God has for you: destiny-level blessings, legacy-level blessings and abundant overflow of health, finances, peace and joy.

> **"The Lord is my strength and my song; He has given me victory." Psalms 118:14**

Everything promised to you is found in the Word of God. Write down the scriptures that you want to see happen in your life on note cards and tape them all around your house, in your car and at your workplace. Decree and declare them over yourself and your children and your finances each and every day.

Speak them in true faith, believing their power and trusting in God that they will manifest in your life. Also remain in good standing with the Lord and in total obedience. You will then begin to see these promises take permanent root in your life and you will see the fruit they produce.

CHAPTER SEVENTEEN
"Daily Decrees and Declarations"

*Is there a difference between reciting biblical
scripture versus decreeing and declaring
it over your life?*

Absolutely!

Reciting scripture means you're repeating it out loud from memory. You are stating and repeating something you've read. This comes from your mind.

Decreeing scripture means you're ordering something to take place with the legal authority given to you through Jesus Christ. It is an official order to the atmosphere, to your angels, and to everything under your authority. This comes from your spirit.

Declaring scripture means you're making a formal announcement and proclamation publically to the spiritual realm. It puts the spiritual realm on notice that something is going to take place regarding a matter of great importance. This comes from your heart.

You should be decreeing and declaring biblical scripture every single day in order to see breakthroughs, upgrades, elevations and promotions in your life.

This is a major key to dreaming BIG and living LARGE!

Once you've designated the scriptures that you need to operate in your life, and you've written them down, you need to begin decreeing and declaring them daily over yourself, over your seed (your children) and over your situation.

Here are some great ones for you to start with in the specific areas you may need, in addition to any of the scriptural verses previously mentioned in each chapter.

In addition to any of the scriptural versus cited throughout this book, I've listed some for you to begin decreeing and declaring daily. They are grouped into 7 different categories depending on your particular needs or situation.

Increase in finances:

> **"Now all glory to God, who is able, through His mighty power at work within us, to accomplish infinitely more than we might ask or think." Ephesians 3:20**

> **"Now this same God who takes care of me will supply all of your needs from His glorious riches, which have been given to us in Christ Jesus." Philippians 4:19**

> **"Your towns and your fields will be blessed." Deuteronomy 28:3**

> **"The Lord will guarantee a blessing on everything you do and will fill your storehouses with grain." Deuteronomy 28:8**

> **"The Lord will send rain at the proper time from His rich treasury in the heavens and will bless all the work you do. You will lend to many nations, but you will never need to borrow from them." Deuteronomy 28:12**

"Bring all the tithes into the storehouses so there will be enough food in my temple. 'If you do, says the Lord of Heaven's Armies, 'I will open the windows of heaven for you. I will pour out a blessing so great you won't have enough room to take it in! Try it! Put me to the test!" Malachi 3:10

"I will end your captivity and restore your fortunes." Jeremiah 29:14

"Restore our fortunes, Lord, as streams renew the desert." Psalms 126:4

Restoration of a marriage or desiring to marry:

"The man who finds a wife finds a treasure, and he receives favor from the Lord." Proverbs 18:22

"Since they are no longer two but one, let no man split apart what God has joined together." Matthew 19:6

"Marriage is for people here on earth." Luke 20:34

"For the believing wife brings holiness to her marriage, and the believing husband brings holiness to his marriage." 1 Corinthians 7:14

"Each man must love his wife as he loves himself, and the wife must respect her husband." Ephesians 5:33

"In this same way, husbands ought to love their wives as they love their own bodies. For a man who loves his wife actually shows love for himself." Ephesians 5:28

"May the Lord bless you with the security of a second marriage." Ruth 1:9

Salvation of those who have turned away from Jesus or who do not know Him:

> "And I will give you a new heart, and I will put a new spirit within you. I will take out your heart of stone and give you a tender, responsive heart." Ezekiel 36:26

> "Create in me a clean heart, O God, and renew a right spirit within me." Psalms 51:10

> "I looked for someone who might rebuild the wall of righteousness that guards the land. I searched for someone to stand in the gap in the wall so I wouldn't have to destroy the land, but I found no one." Ezekiel 22:30

Blessings of favor over your children and wanting to have children:

> "Your children and your crops will be blessed. The offspring of your herds and flocks will be blessed." Deuteronomy 28:4

> "Direct your children onto the right path, and when they are older, they will not leave it." Proverbs 22:6

> "The children of your people will live in security. Their children's children will thrive in your presence." Psalms 102:28

> "May the Lord richly bless you and your children." Psalms 115:14

> "But the love of the Lord remains forever with those who fear Him. His salvation extends to the children's children." Psalms 103:17

> "You will have many children; your descendants will be as plentiful as grass!" Job 5:25

"Then God remembered Rachel's plight and answered her prayers by enabling her to have children."
Genesis 30:22

When you are in need of protection:

"No weapon formed against me shall prosper."
Isaiah 54:17

"O Lord, I have come to you for protection; don't let me be disgraced." **Psalms 71:1**

"My life is an example to many because you have been my strength and protection." **Psalms 71:7**

"I come to you for protection, O Lord my God. Save me from persecutors – rescue me!" **Psalms 7:1**

"Every Word of God proves true. He is a shield to all who come to Him for protection." **Proverbs 30:5**

"Pull me from the trap my enemies set for me, for I find protection in you alone." **Psalms 31:4**

"He will cover you with His feathers. He will shelter you with His wings. His faithful promises are your armor and protection." **Psalms 91:4**

"My God is my rock, in whom I find protection. He is my shield, the power that saves me, and my place of safety. He is my refuge, my savior, the one who saves me from violence." **2 Samuel 22:3**

Success and favor in your career, business, ministry or calling:

"Oh that you would bless me and expand my territory! Please be with me in all that I do, and keep me from all troubles and pain!" 1 Chronicles 4:10

"Please Lord, please save us. Please, Lord, please give us success." Psalms 118:25

"I cry out to the God Most High, to God who will fulfill His purpose for me." Psalms 57:2

"You can make many plans, but the Lord's purpose will prevail." Proverbs 19:21

"Wherever you go and whatever you do will be blessed." Deuteronomy 28:6

"I will make you in to a great nation. I will bless you and make you famous, and you will be a blessing to others." Genesis 12:2

When you are in need of physical or emotional healing:

"But He was pierced for our rebellion, crushed for our sins. He was beaten so we could be whole. He was whipped so we could be healed." Isaiah 53:5

"And He said to her, 'Daughter, your faith has made you well. Go in peace. Your suffering is over." Mark 5:34

"He forgives all my sins and heals all my diseases." Psalms 103:3

"He heals the brokenhearted and bandages their wounds." Psalms 147:3

"Then you will have healing for your body and strength for your bones." Proverbs 3:8

"By His wounds, you are healed." 1 Peter 2:24

Remember to be careful not to deactivate the power of these scriptures as you are decreeing and declaring them by being disobedient. Breaking spiritual laws will allow the enemy to accuse you in the heavenly court.

"One day, the members of the heavenly court came to present themselves before the Lord, and the accuser, satan, came with them." Job 1:6

If the accusations against you are accurate, then all of your work to gain favor, elevation and breakthrough may be blocked by the consequences of your own actions.

Just as there is accountability for breaking laws in the natural world, there is also accountability for breaking laws in the spiritual world. The judgment in the heavenly court rendered either against us or in our favor directly affects what we see happening in the natural world.

This is why it's so important to understand how the spiritual judicial system works and is structured.

CHAPTER EIGHTEEN

"Spiritual Laws and the Heavenly Court"

Do you know that the court system
we have here on earth mirrors the
one in heaven? Did you even know that
there is a court system m heaven?

In heaven as is here on earth, there is a judicial system that interprets and applies the law of the Kingdom. The Kingdom of God is not some abstract place of nothingness where we will float up to when we die and do nothing for eternity. It is a genuine world-ruling government, led by God Laws and boundaries which are upheld in the heavenly court system. Heaven's law system holds jurisdiction here on earth, as well.

These laws are ruled on in the spiritual realm, but the "court orders" affect the natural world. They activate angelic activity to release blessings to us, and they constrain demons from doing what their superior, satan, has ordered them to do against us.

Things of the world that can be seen in the natural are directly affected by angels and demons. Money flow can be stopped, hindered or increased. Disease can be afflicted upon the human body or eliminated from it in healing. Storms can be initiated, redirected or stopped. Internet activity, phones and cable connections can all be interfered with, slowed down or restored back to full function.

Even though all of these things can be affected, understand that God is still in complete control of everything and always will be. So anything that an angel does only takes place at the command of God. Everything a demon does is ordered to it by satan but can only be carried out if it is allowed by God. God will only allow demonic attack as a direct result of a court ruling in the Heavenly Court. Satan is not free to run around doing whatever he wants to do. He must be given legal permission by God.

Of course, he doesn't play by the rules, and this shouldn't surprise anyone. He rebelled against God and was cast out of heaven, so he rebels against God's laws, too.

> **"And the dragon lost the battle, and he and his angles were forced out of heaven." Revelation 12:7**

He often attacks people illegally, without following spiritual law, and he's never going to stop doing this. The same thing happens on earth with people who don't follow laws. Drug dealers still buy and sell drugs even though it's illegal and destroys lives. Bank robbers still rob banks. People still kill. These acts actually mirror satan's 3 part agenda to steal, kill and destroy. In fact, it is satan who is responsible for these crimes taking place by influencing the offender to corrupt them.

Just as physical crimes on earth are litigated in the courts and court rulings (punishments) are granted for or against the criminal, spiritual crimes are litigated in the Heavenly Court and rulings are made in favor of or against the offender, or sinner.

It has existed since before the earth was even created.

> **"When the Most High assigned lands to the nations, when He divided up the human race, He established boundaries of the peoples according to the number in His heavenly court." Deuteronomy 32:8**

The Heavenly Court is setup just like courts here on earth. But it is the earthly court that mirrors the heavenly one, not the other way around. The courts on earth took their structural ideas out of biblical scripture.

Here, there is a judge, a defense attorney and a prosecuting attorney. The Judge makes the ruling, or legally-binding decision, on a case against a potential offender. The accused is represented by a defense attorney who pleads the case to the judge trying to attain a ruling of innocence for the accused. The accuser is represented by a prosecuting attorney who pleads the case in an effort to get a ruling of guilty against the accused with a punishment attached to it.

All of this was taken from scripture which describes and details the structure of the Heavenly Court. God, the Most High, is the judge of the universe. He judges the Heavens and the Earth. He is the ruling judge of Heaven's Court.

> **"God presides over heaven's court; He pronounces judgment on the heavenly beings." Psalms 82:1**

Jesus is the Mediator between us and the Father. So He is our defense attorney, pleading our case before God. He works tirelessly to help us. He wants us to be found innocent of whatever the enemy accuses us of doing. So, He mediates on our behalf and represents us in the Heavenly Court before God and the enemy.

> **"For, there is one God and one Mediator who can reconcile God and humanity – the man Christ Jesus." 1 Timothy 2:5**

Satan is both the accuser and the persecuting attorney. He is relentlessly working to bring accusations of sin to God in order to get rulings against us.

> **"The accuser, satan, was there at the angel's right hand, making accusations against Jeshua." Zechariah 3:1**

Satan knows that God is a just and fair God. So he often tricks us in to sin on a technicality, and then goes straight to God with it. God will order against us, if we are in the wrong, despite how deeply He loves us. He is no respecter of persons. What is fair for one is fair for all.

The enemy knows this. He also knows scripture backwards and forwards. So, we must be careful to obey God's commands as He has spoken them.

> **"All He does is just and good, and all His commandments are trustworthy."**
> **Psalms 111:7**

God's commands are laid out very clearly throughout the Old and New Testaments of His Word. The Ten Commandments, in the book of Exodus, are rules that God commands us to obey.

> **"You must not have any other God before me.**
>
> **You must not make for yourself an idol or image of any kind or an image of anything in the heavens or on the earth or in the sea. You must not bow down to them or worship them, for I, the Lord your God, am a jealous God who will not tolerate your affection for any other gods. I lay the sins of the parents upon their children; the entire family is affected – even children in the third and fourth generations of those who reject me. But I lavish unfailing love for a thousand generations on those who love me and obey my commands.**
>
> **You must not misuse the name of the Lord your God. The Lord will not let you go unpunished if you misuse His name.**
>
> **Remember to observe the Sabbath day by keeping it holy. You have six days each week for your ordinary work, but the seventh day is a Sabbath day of rest dedicated to the Lord your God. On that day, no one**

in your household may do any work. This includes you, your sons and daughters, your male and female servants, your livestock, and any foreigners living among you. For in six days the Lord made the heavens, the earth, the sea and everything in them, but on the seventh day, He rested. That is why the Lord blessed the Sabbath day and set it apart as holy.

Honor your father and mother. Then you will live a long, full life in the land the Lord your God is giving you.

You must not murder.

Yon must not commit adultery.

You must not steal.

You must not testify falsely against your neighbor.

You must not covet your neighbor's house. You must not covet your neighbor's wife, male or female servant, ox, donkey, or anything else that belongs to your neighbor."

Exodus 20:2-17

The Ten Commandments aren't the only rules that God commands us to obey. The rest of His commands are spread throughout His Word. Some of the other commands God gives us may be less obvious as being sin. God commands us not to fear anything, not to worry about anything and never to doubt Him. Unbelief is also a sin, as well as premarital sex, watching porn (even watching sex scenes in a regular movie), gossiping, judging others, unforgiveness, unrepentance, pride, arrogance, selfishness, blasphemy and disobedience to the Lord.

Sin isn't merely breaking some christian rule inside the bible, and then afterwards, going about your business and living your life as usual. Sin is a transgression of divine law that has serious consequences in both the natural and the spiritual realms.

In the natural, sin can land you in prison, limit your freedom with community-hour obligations, restrict your traveling rights, result in job/career loss, strip you of a professional license, or cause you to be blackballed.

In the spiritual realm, sin can give the enemy legal rights to your finances, your marriage, your family members, your job, your body, or your mind. When the enemy has legal rights to you, he sends reinforcements (demon gangs made up of several demons) to outnumber and overwhelm you, in hopes of getting you to the point of no return.

The point of no return is the damnation of your soul. This eternal consequence is his main objective and goal. You see, he definitely enjoys torturing people while they're here on earth, but what he really wants is for them to join him in hell for eternity and keep them permanently separated from God like he is. Satan knows what his destiny is and where he's going to end up, so as a final revenge towards God for kicking him out of heaven forever, he wants to take as many people with him to hell as he possibly can.

The only problem for him is that he cannot change your destiny or cancel it because he did not create it. God created it. He cannot create anything, unlike God. But what he CAN do is trick you or otherwise influence you to sin without repentance because then you will alter your own destiny and face the same eternal consequences that satan will. That's a win for him!

So you must understand the laws and how the Heavenly Court system works in order to avoid serious and eternal consequences. I'm convinced that if everyone understood all of this, the world would be a much different place.

If you sin, you will undoubtedly be accused by satan in court. God will judge you based on the facts. If you're guilty, then you're guilty. There's no gray area with God. God is Light, and He is Truth. He is a good Father, a fair Father, and a promise keeper.

"The Lord is just! He is my rock! There is no evil in Him!" Psalms 92:15

All of the spiritual laws that exist are in the Word. But you don't need to stress about remembering all of them because the Holy Spirit will give a check in your spirit, or a "funny" feeling in your stomach when you're about to make the decision to sin. You'll know what to do and what to say because He will tell you. He is our Helper. One of His jobs is to help guide us and keep us on the path of righteousness.

It's also important to know that the basis of every single one of God's spiritual laws is simply to love Jesus.

"I love God's law with all my heart." Romans 7:21

So if you sincerely and passionately love Him with all your heart, then you will not break His laws because you won't want to offend or hurt Him any way. By loving Him, you'll love everyone else too and you will not break His law.

"We know we love God's children if we love God and obey His commandments." 1 John 5:2

If you do slip up, just repent right away and you will still see His favor and blessings in your life. Remember that you are of a royal priesthood bloodline.

"But you are not like that, for you are a chosen people. You are royal priests, a holy nation, God's very own possession. As a result, you can show others the goodness of God, for He called you out of the darkness into HIS wonderful Light." 1 Peter 2:9

You were created to be financially stable, to be healthy and happy and to be dreaming BIG and living LARGE!

I speak tremendous favor over your life. Excellent health, long life, great wealth, happiness, joy, prominence and prosperity are your inheritance and your portion They shall be yours and it shall not be otherwise in Jesus' precious and all-powerful name. God bless you in a mighty way on the journey to your God-ordained destiny!

ABOUT THE AUTHOR

Dr. Kathleen Abate is a passionate servant and believer in Jesus Christ. In 2011, she began using the gifts God had given her as an advanced general dentist for the Kingdom by transitioning her dental practice from a 100% traditional business to shared time providing free dental care to those in need. She treated homeless men and women from a soup kitchen in Detroit, as well as women and children from a local domestic violence center. She knew in her heart she had to use what God had given her to bless others.

Over the next 5 years, Dr. Abate began helping others in the community as well. She met a man who had contracted Hepatitis from volunteering to clean up rubble following the 2005 Hurricane Katrina natural disaster. He was in need of a liver transplant, but couldn't get on the transplant list until all of his teeth were extracted. However, his medical bills had left him penniless. So Dr. Abate extracted all of his teeth and made him dentures free of charge.

Her television debut came shortly after that when she volunteered to gift a Detroit man with a complete smile makeover. He struggled financially and couldn't find a job because of the condition of his teeth. The complete transformation of his smile makeover was taped and televised as a two-part series on a local Detroit news station, WXYZ Detroit.

Dr. Abate's philanthropy continued to evolve over time. She began driving around Detroit with her staff and personally distributing food and blankets to homeless men and women, as well as, sending bibles and oral health care kits to domestic violence centers.

She then discovered that there was a need for help in other areas as well. Hundreds of disabled and homeless US Veterans in Ann Arbor, Michigan were in need of complete dental restoration. So she founded Hope's Smile, a 501c3 non-profit ministerial foundation, in January 2017 to further expand her ministry.

Hope's Smile Ministries
(www.hopessmile.us)

She also founded an online non-profit store selling t-shirts and other items for the ministry in March 2018.

Hope's Smile Online Store
(www.hopessmile-store.us)

Today, she continues to bless those in need by doing all of what she started. She has also expanded her outreach program to include One-on-One Spiritual Mentoring to guide others toward advancement in their walk with Jesus Christ.

She has a true passion in her heart for anyone who struggles emotionally, physically, financially or spiritually because she understands how it feels to struggle She also wants to share with you how to get all that God has for you!

This book will empower you to change your life forever.

Dr. Kathleen Abate learned everything in this book first hand from God. She went through a divine process of personal and spiritual transformation led by Jesus Christ and became a fearless warrior for Him.

She wants the same thing to happen for you!

"May Almighty God bless every person who reads this book with a divine prosperity that completely transforms every area of your life!"

Dr. Kathleen Abate

Printed in the United States
By Bookmasters